HULTON'S PICTURE HISTORIES

GENERAL EDITOR: SIR EDWARD HULTON

Furniture

The Dean and Chapter, St. Paul's Cathedral

Bishop Compton's Chair. Carved walnut. Not later than 1710.

A Picture History of

Furniture

Frank Davis

Edward Hulton

London

First published 1958 by

E. HULTON AND COMPANY LIMITED

161-166 Fleet Street, London, E.C.4

Printed in Great Britain by

Hills & Lacy Ltd.

Watford and London

Contents

Introduction and Acknowledgments

This book contains one man's selection of four hundred photographs to illustrate changing fashions in furniture. The emphasis is mainly on England and France, with occasional excursions to China, Italy and Spain. Both types and many of the individual pieces will be familiar enough, and a considerable number have passed through the London auction rooms in recent years. A fair proportion, whether in national or private collections can be classed as indubitable masterpieces, but I have endeavoured to include among them certain agreeable run-of-the-mill pieces which are fair examples of their kind without being exceptional. Whenever I turn over the pages of a book of this character I invariably ask myself why on earth such and such a favourite piece has been omitted, and I have no doubt that many readers will experience a similar disappointment. The answer is that, surprising as it may seem at first sight, one soon discovers that to include everything one would like to include would involve well over a thousand examples—far beyond the scope of this publication. Experienced collectors will find nothing much that is new to them in the following pages. What I have attempted is to provide beginners with a comprehensive survey of a very wide field and to limit comment to essentials. As far as I am aware the marked differences between Chinese furniture and what Europe fondly imagined was Chinese furniture have not been illustrated previously in any other publication of this kind; nor, to the best of my knowledge, has the beautiful 15th century Flemish drawing (Fig. 4) of the stools and chairs which I saw at the exhibition at Paris in the Orangerie of the Robert Lehman collection in 1957. I am particularly grateful to Mr. Lehman for permission to reproduce this drawing, as important as a document as it is æsthetically, and to the many private owners (some of whom have allowed their names to appear beneath the photographs) who have so willingly allowed me to illustrate their treasured possessions. I also wish to record my grateful thanks for advice and for every possible help to the Directors of Christie's and of Sothebys', to other auctioneers and to Mr. L. G. G. Ramsey, Editor of the *Connoisseur*. I am also greatly indebted to my many friends among the antique dealers. We are so accustomed to whole-hearted assistance from officials at The Victoria and Albert Museum, that most lively repository of magnificence and learning, that we are tempted to take it for granted—as my debt to them increases daily on many counts, let me assure them that I, for one, do not. I must also express my thanks to the President and Fellows of Queens' College, Cambridge, for permission to illustrate the Erasmus Chair (Fig. 6); to the Master and Fellows of Magdalene College, Cambridge, for the photograph of the Samuel Pepys desk (Fig. 95); to the Dean and Chapter of Exeter Cathedral for the photograph of the chair in the Bishop's Throne (Fig. 42) and to the Dean and Chapter of St. Paul's for the photograph of Bishop Compton's chair which provides the frontispiece.

In many cases the present whereabouts of the fine things illustrated, particularly those which have passed through the London auction rooms in recent years, is unknown; a fair proportion of them will have long since crossed either the Channel or the Atlantic. I can only hope that their present owners, if they should happen to recognise them in these pages, will not be displeased; they are there because I think them worthwhile and for no other reason. I have been cautious about dating for the obvious reason that styles overlap and fashions started at court take time to permeate downwards. Beginners therefore will not conclude that as soon as, for example, Queen Anne ascended the throne what, with our hind-sight, we call conveniently the Queen Anne style emerged in its characteristic sobriety any more than the inhabitants of Florence woke up some centuries earlier and said "Let's start the Renaissance." Labels help us to keep our minds tidy, but they do no more than that. They are the most valuable of servants, but make very poor masters.

I *Westminster Abbey*

The Coronation Chair. Carved oak, with traces of original paint.

Preliminaries

A LONG TIME AGO

Wood, in all its variety, is a singularly beautiful material and at the same time so familiar that we rarely look at it closely. Still less, as a rule, do we pay overmuch attention to the affectionate ingenuity with which man has, at certain moments in his history, coaxed it rather than forced it into shapes which seemed to him comely by the standards of his time. Perhaps a dozen or so—possibly more—of the pieces of furniture illustrated in the following pages come into the category of unfortunate aberrations; one or two of them I would cheerfully label horror-comics. But yet this is certain; they were much admired in their day, and it seemed a pity to omit them just because the majority of my generation would not willingly give them house room. If any experts look through this book they will have little difficulty in noting many omissions of this or that type. I plead guilty without more ado, and merely remark in extenuation that to include everything would have meant doubling or trebling the size of the volume and decreasing the size of the illustrations. Moreover this is not intended to be an encyclopædia but a pictorial history which will provide the non-expert with a fair notion of what happened without overmuch detail. There is a good deal about the 17th century and much more about the 18th because, both in France and England, far more from that period has survived and the skill of the cabinetmaker reached such heights. At the same time, it is well to be reminded that high standards of craftsmanship had been known previously—hence the photograph of Tutankhamen's Throne, as fine a piece of imaginative workmanship as anything Europe in its heyday managed to produce. This is of course an important ceremonial piece of furniture, its decoration determined by religious considerations. Perhaps it is not outrageous to set beside it the marvellously carved red lacquer 18th century throne of the

Emperor of China, Ch'ien Lung (A.D. 1736-1795) or our own imposing if far less sophisticated Coronation chair—three pieces so far apart in time and style that they might come, not from different places on the earth, but from different planets, so various is man's activity. Yet types persist very little changed for centuries, as witness the turned chairs, illustrated first by an early sculpture, next by a Flemish drawing which can be dated to about 1445, then by the beautifully proportioned chair from Queens' College, Cambridge, associated with the distinguished name of Erasmus, and finally by the sturdy early 19th century country-made chair with its spindle back and rush seat. Similar things are made today, so that we have in these illustrations quite definite proof of a continuity stretching back for at least eight hundred years. The drawing finds a place here because of the stools and chairs to be seen in it. There is an X stool on the left of the sort we associate vaguely with churches, then a three-legged stool with a triangular seat; another X stool, a chair and two other three-legged triangular seated stools can be distinguished. Some explanation of so peculiar a drawing seems to be called for. In the popular slang of the period, to sweep up chairs and stools into a chaotic heap signified social disorder—to agitate, to start a revolution. The drawing is believed to be a design for one of the capitals of the Hôtel de Ville at Brussels and was intended to symbolise the advantages gained by the various trades of the city as a result of their long struggle for what, at that time, was a highly democratic system of self-government. The type of chair illustrated in so dignified a manner by the Erasmus

3 *Victoria & Albert Museum*

The Throne of the Emperor Ch'ien Lung. 18th century, carved red lacquer.

chair, became popular also in America, where a fair number have survived. One, in the Pilgrim Hall, Plymouth, is popularly supposed to have been brought over by Elder Brewster in the *Mayflower*. Those who have seen the recent replica of the *Mayflower* will have no difficulty in deciding that in so crowded and so small a vessel a chair of this sort was a most unlikely piece of furniture. Nor have we any record that Erasmus himself ever used the chair to which his name is given, though it is easy enough to understand how the College from a very early date, would associate the name of so distinguished a visitor with a chair which was quite likely to have been there when he arrived. Naturally such pieces, unless preserved carefully by pious hands, are not likely to survive the ordinary hazards of rough usage—which makes it all the more remarkable that two small turned chairs of very simple construction, which have always been known as "Henry VIII" chairs and certainly date from the 16th century still exist at Westminster School.

How much has perished? We shall never know, but clearly we owe the survival of the Egyptian throne to the dryness of the climate and the chance that robbers were unable to discover the entrance to the tomb. Of Greek, of Roman, of Byzantine furniture, ceremonial or otherwise, we possess only metal fragments; from the ancient Chinese tombs, only more or less imperishable materials—bronzes, jades and pottery. Wood is subject to every kind of disaster: fire, water, insects; and even today, unless reasonably well looked after, can almost disintegrate behind our backs. We can consider ourselves fortunate that the Coronation Chair in Westminster Abbey has not long since succumbed to vandals; of its original gilding and painting only trivial traces remain, and it is dreadfully disfigured by initials cut into the back. None the less, apart from its very special national significance, it remains a noble piece of

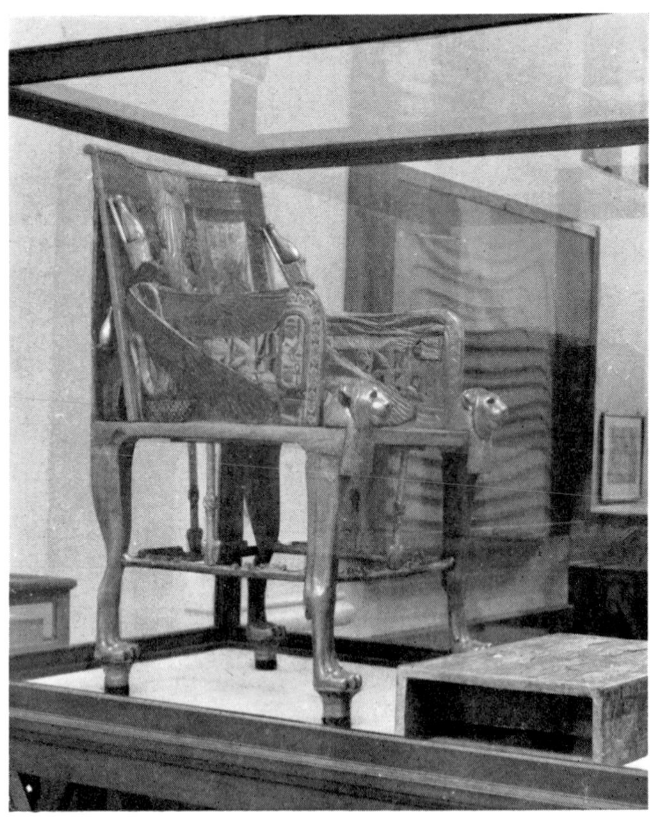

2 *Cairo Museum*

The Throne of Tutankhamen.

4 *Lehman Collection, New York*

SWEEPING UP THE STOOLS

This beautiful drawing by an anonymous Flemish master of about the year 1445 is probably a design for one of the capitals of the Hôtel de Ville at Brussels. Its intrinsic merit as a drawing is obvious and demands no further comment in a book of this character. Its interest for the connoisseur of furniture lies in the evidence it provides of the type of ordinary chairs and stools familiar in Flanders during the 15th century. The curious and obscure subject is explained by the suggestion that, in common parlance, "to mix up stools and chairs" signified social chaos, chairs representing top people and stools their inferiors. Thus, a capital on the Town Hall carved to this design would point to the advantages gained by the struggle of the various trades to achieve a democratic constitution.

work, the same in essentials as when it was executed in oak by Master Walter, the King's Painter, about the year 1301.

Another chair of ceremony, not so august nor so ancient, has been chosen as the frontispiece to this volume. It is noticed by few, but deserves to be numbered among the finest things of its age and country. It was made for Bishop Compton, who was Bishop of London when St. Paul's was rededicated in 1710 and is a superb example of wood carving combined with a beautiful balance in the design as a whole—at once rich in detail and dignified in form. From its style alone one would be tempted to place it during the later years of the 17th century rather than the beginning of the 18th; and indeed it may well have been designed long before it was placed in the cathedral. But ecclesiastical furniture obeys its own laws—or at least can hardly be expected to conform to the changing fashions of the polite world—and this magnificent chair was very likely made only a year or so before the opening ceremony. That is, it probably seemed already old-fashioned to the subjects of Queen Anne who thronged the cathedral on that occasion.

Another and an earlier chair, beautifully restored after years of neglect—a secular chair, now in Exeter Cathedral as the seat in the Bishop's Throne—is illustrated later (Fig. 42).

5 *The Louvre*

St. Matthew writing his Gospel. 12th century carving from Chartres.

6 *The President and Fellows, Queen's College, Cambridge*

The Erasmus Chair. Early 16th century.

7

A 19th century Turned Chair.

8 *Metropolitan Museum, New York*

An "Elder Brewster" Chair.

To the End of the Sixteenth Century

Our forefathers were probably a good deal ruder than we care to acknowledge. Such a simple and, one would imagine, obvious amenity as a table fork seems to have been as great a rarity in 16th century France as in 16th century England ; it did not become common in either country until well into the 17th century, and even then was probably regarded in conservative circles as just one more of those effeminate Italian fads. Not without reason was Italy saluted later as the Mother of the Arts. This book is not concerned with small table utensils, but the circumstance is worth mentioning because it serves to illustrate a point which I think is brought out very clearly by some of the early Italian cabinets and chests to be seen in the following pages—that Italy was at least a century ahead of us in the graces of life. These painted or carved chests and cabinets with their carvings and elaborate interior arrangements must have seemed astonishing to people accustomed to a simpler mode of life—and simple this life was even in great houses; a table (often on trestles), a bench or two, possibly a chair for the head of the family, two or three chests—a cypress wood chest is mentioned in 1397 in John o' Gaunt's will—and a bed which would be a wooden framework with linen or velvet hangings. That would be the extent of the furnishings in the houses of the well-to-do while the less prosperous would make do with even rougher appointments. Practically nothing has survived in England earlier than about 1500 except a few chests, and those mostly in churches, and one or two other rare objects such as the cradle to be seen in the London Museum which tradition asserts was once the cradle of Henry V but which would appear from its style to have been made much later in the 15th century. By the 16th century Flanders and France, already fairly mature in the major crafts, were beginning to influence the comparatively backward subjects of the Tudor monarchy and we have to admit that, however much we may disapprove of so unpleasant a Renaissance prince as Henry VIII, both he and his formidable daughter Elizabeth served their country well by encouraging Flemish, French and Italian craftsmen to settle here. The strangers were not welcomed—indeed there is ample evidence that they were cordially disliked—but in the long run their special skills set the standard for glass, for ceramics, for clockmaking, and for furniture alike. A great deal of furniture was imported from Flanders—commercial contacts had been close for centuries—and when the style of the Renaissance at last reached our shores, it came at second hand about the middle of the century and was interpreted in a decidedly clumsy manner—great bulbous legs for tables, and masks and terminal figures and grotesques for cupboards and chimney pieces and bed boards. Instead of the earlier linenfold chest you find, until well into the 17th century, elaborately arched panels inlaid with floral inlay and separated by carved terminal figures of men and women. Inlay is the term used to describe a pattern of various woods and/or bone or ivory set into the solid. Marquetry (or parquetry) demands far more skill and comes much later, in the second half of the 17th century. A popular type of inlaid chest was that known as the None-such, in which the front is inlaid with a stylised architectural design, popularly supposed to be derived from Henry VIII's great palace at Cheam. This building evidently made the strongest possible impression upon the Elizabethan imagination, possibly, it has been suggested, because it seemed to symbolise the country's growing prosperity and importance. It was built by Henry VIII from the designs of the Italian del Nunziata, was seen and described by both Samuel Pepys and John Evelyn, and, in 1670, was bestowed by Charles II upon my Lady Castlemaine—who demolished it. It is however doubtful whether the design of this inlay originated in England ; it seems to have been fairly common in Germany and many such chests were probably imported or were the work of immigrants. The most lively survey of the general standard of life in Elizabethan times is provided by William Harrison whose *Description of England* was published in 1587 with Holinshed's *Chronicle*. He sums up as follows " The furniture of our houses is grown in manner even to passing delicacy; and herein I do not speak of the nobility and gentry only, but likewise of the lowest sort. Certes in noblemen's houses it is not rare to see abundance of arras, rich hangings of tapestry, silver vessels and so much other plate as may furnish sundry cupboards "—(he refers to *cup boards*—the tiers of open shelves for the display of plate ; our ancestors liked to advertise their wealth)—" to the sum of-ten-times of a thousand or two thousand pounds at the least, whereby the value of this and the rest of their stuff doth grow to be almost inestimable ". He goes on to speak of the tapestry, Turkey work (i.e. carpets, much in favour for table coverings, as in

Holbein's great painting " The Ambassadors " in The National Gallery), pewter, brass, fine linen, belonging to lesser men, and continues : " But, as herein all these sorts do far exceed their elders and predecessors, so in times past the costly furniture stayed there, whereas now it is descended yet lower, even into the inferior artificers and many farmers who have, for the most part, learned also to garnish their cupboards with plate, their joined beds " (i.e. beds made by a joiner, not roughly put together by a carpenter) " with tapestry and silk hangings, and their tables with carpets and fine napery, whereby the wealth of our country doth infinitely appear". It is noticeable here that the emphasis is on textiles and plate, not upon furniture, which was evidently regarded as of small interest in itself. The main wood used was oak, with a good deal of ash or elm; walnut was by no means unknown for the finest pieces, nor was chestnut, of which a very interesting example at Aston Hall, Birmingham, is illustrated. Turned chairs and stools of yew and other native woods had been popular for generations, and were by no means confined to England. In a carving from the Cathedral at Chartres, now in the Louvre, St. Matthew is seen writing his gospel seated on a chair of this sort, and the remarkable Flemish drawing of about 1445 already mentioned provides clear proof that such pieces of furniture were common. An inventory of the contents of Arundel Castle taken in 1580 lists the following: in the long gallery, six inlaid walnut chairs, three chairs covered with black leather, six joined stools, an inlaid square framed table and a walnut cupboard. In the great hall were eight trestle tables (two of them fir), two chairs, two joined forms and sixteen " Stools of waynescotte " (i.e. joined stools). There were many wall hangings and Turkey carpets. Of these carpets one was placed on each of the cupboards. Panelled joined chairs with turned legs and open arms began to find favour about the middle of the century, and, not unnaturally, have survived in greater numbers than upholstered pieces. The so-called court cupboard—the term has nothing to do with the Royal Court, but is simply the French—*court:* short—could be open or could contain a canted central closed cupboard in the upper part. It was in essentials a stand in three stages ; the transition to a fully closed cupboard or press is obvious enough. The livery cupboard was used for containing food, its front pierced to admit air, and was made to hang on a wall; it can be considered as the very primitive ancestor of the modern refrigerator.

It is perhaps worth noting that the French word for furniture is *mobilier*—that is, when the word came into use furniture was regarded as in fact mobile, not just in the sense of being movable from room to room, but from place to place. Important people in Europe were incorrigible travellers and, when trekking from one great mansion to another, would take with them not merely clothes but the complete appointments of a house. This is not to say that there were no monumental beds and cabinets too clumsy to move, but that, up to the end of the 16th century, a great deal of the furniture was made in such a way that it could be packed up and transported with comparative ease. It is clear from the 1589 inventory of Catherine de Medici that, with rare exceptions, her possessions could be taken to pieces. Tapestries and hangings would be taken down from the walls, beds and chairs and tables dismembered and then the whole stowed away in great cases. Even as late as 1624 the room of the Duchess of Lorraine contains six chairs and a walnut table which could be taken apart, a close-stool which could be packed in three parts, and twelve folding chairs, while in 1599 the inventory of Gabrielle d'Estrées describes a bed with turned walnut posts which, with all its accessories, could be stowed in two leather trunks and two linen containers. Perhaps we can say that the 16th century marks the beginning of the end of this peripatetic furniture fashion. Great personages still moved about, but more settled conditions and a gradual improvement in material wealth and comfort made these makeshift arrangements unnecessary. None the less most rooms—whether those of the very rich or the merely moderately affluent—continued to be sparely furnished by modern standards.

Apart from the fine cabinets already mentioned, for which Italy set the standard, it is not possible to speak of the furniture of this and earlier centuries without particular reference to the chests (*cassoni*) which are among the most splendid things springing from Italian soil which have come down to us. As with us—and indeed with every other country—they were as often as not marriage coffers to contain the bride's trousseau, but in Italy they attained a distinction to which none else aspired. It was second nature to an Italian to cover any suitable space with painting, and the sides of these great chests, in the fifteenth century and later, were frequently used as vehicles for the most delightful pictures. Many of these paintings survive in their original positions, but when they do not they are treasured as works of art in their own right, appear in sales of Old Masters and are no less appreciatively received than works by the painters of altarpieces or of portraits. Such treatment of a piece of furniture was wholly beyond the imagination of Northern peoples; not that we did not sometimes decorate furniture with colours, but we did not treat it pictorially. Another technique in which Italy was far in advance of the rest of us was in the use of gesso—that is chalk worked into a paste with parchment size and carved in low relief, by which the most delicate effects could be obtained. It was a technique well known in Florence by the end of the 15th century; with us it was not used until about 1690 and enjoyed a brief popularity for about 30 years. Apart from that, the normal material for an Italian chest was walnut, for Northern Europe oak—the former a softer wood and more amenable to sculptural subtleties. Add to all this a far more consciously learned classical tradition and it is hardly surprising that the average carved coffer from France or Flanders or England which can be dated as early as the 16th century seems a trifle provincial by comparison.

9

Victoria & Albert Museum

9. Carved oak Chest. French, 14th century. A tournament.

10. Front Panel of a gilded and painted chest. Italian, late 15th century.

11. Painted walnut Chest. Italian, 14th century.

10

Victoria & Albert Museum

11

Victoria & Albert Museum

12. Mediæval Bedroom, from a 15th century Flemish MS.

13. Painted Altar Chest.

14. Oak Stool. English, early 16th century. Shaped and splayed board ends and pierced apron piece.

15. Oak long Stool. English, 16th century. Shaped trestle ends, champered edge, shaped long rails and protruding checks.

13 *Newport, Essex*

14 *S. W. Wolsey*

15 *Mr. R. T. Gwynn*

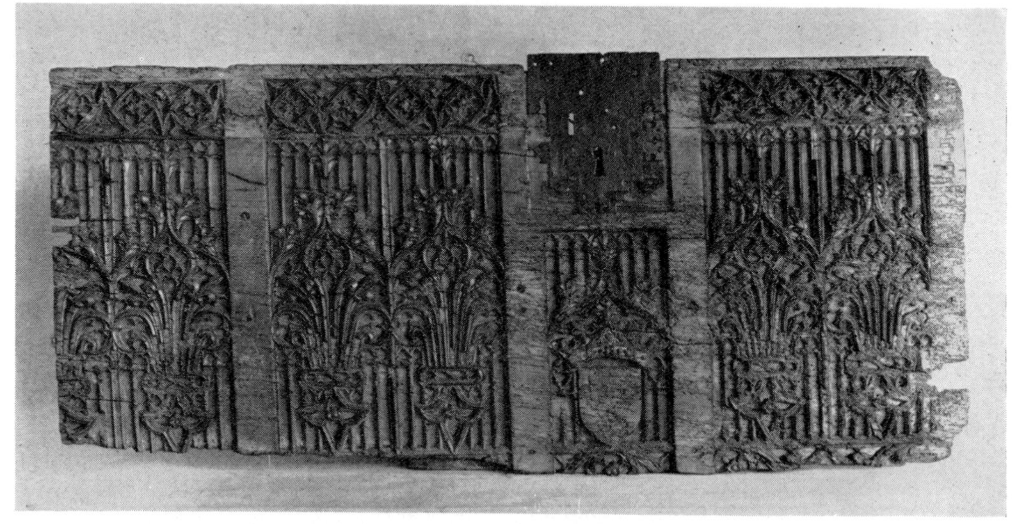

16 *The Victoria & Albert Museum*

17 *S. W. Wolsey*

16. Carved oak Panel – the front of a chest. Delicate Gothic tracery. French, end of 14th century.

17. Carved oak Chair. French, 16th century.

18. Oak Chair. English, 16th century. Carved and with floral inlay in centre of arcaded back.

18 *Victoria & Albert Museum*

19

Mrs. Geoffrey Hart

Oak court or plate cupboard. English, late 16th century.

20 *Christchurch Mansion, Ipswich*
Oak Cupboard with linenfold panels. English, 16th century.

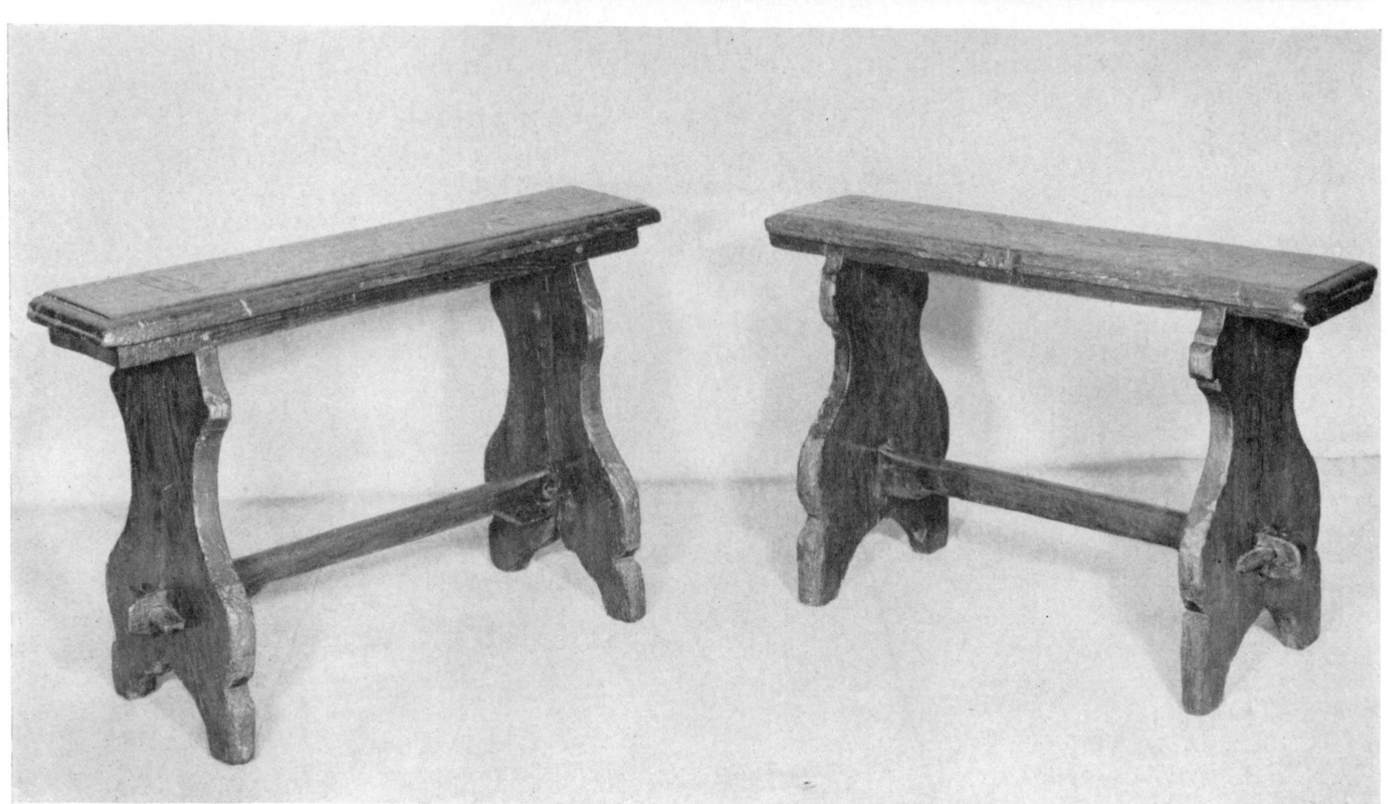

21 *S. W. Wolsey*
Two small Benches. Northern French, early 16th century. Thick top with recessed moulded edge. Shaped trestle and supports with tie bars and tongued ends.

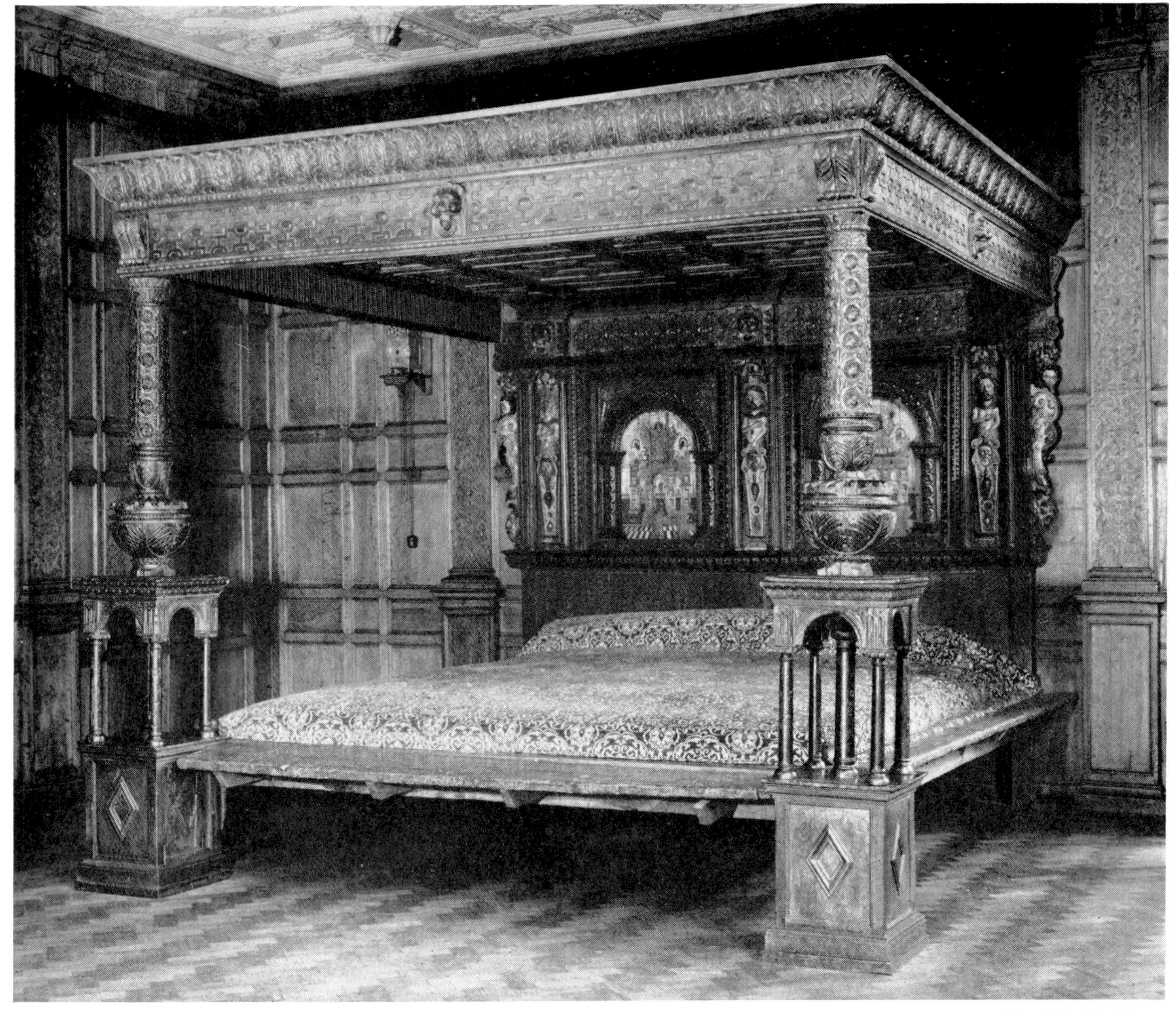

Victoria & Albert Museum

Carved oak. The Great Bed of Ware, 16th century.

THE GREAT BED OF WARE

This remarkable but to modern eyes scarcely beautiful piece of carved oak furniture seems to have become a legend almost as soon as it was made during the reign of Elizabeth I, which possibly accounts for its survival when others of the same type have long since disappeared. It is not known for what great house it was originally designed, though it is hardly likely that its first owner was an innkeeper. For many years it was a considerable attraction at the Crown Inn at Ware in Hertfordshire, where Sir Henry Chauncey, early in the 18th century, was fascinated by its unusual size, and relates how " six citizens and their wives " came one day from London, and " for a frolick " were all accommodated in the Great Bed. Shakespeare refers to it in *Twelfth Night*—" a sheet big enough for the Bed of Ware in England "—while an allusion in Ben Johnson's " Silent Woman " (1609) indicates that it was already a familiar jest on the stage. The German traveller Paul Hentzner mentions that several beds of almost the same dimensions were shown to him at Windsor Castle in 1598, so that it is possible that, for a time at least, our Elizabethan ancestors, who rarely did things by halves, had persuaded themselves that beds of gargantuan proportions were convincing evidence of prosperity. 19th century romanticism, nourished upon the novels of Sir Walter Scott, could not be expected to accept so late a date as the reign of Elizabeth for so famous, indeed so fabulous a bed, consequently—probably early in the century—some well intentioned antiquarian carved the date 1463 upon it, one of the many examples of the way in which people prefer foolish fiction to fact.

The height is 8 ft., the width 10 ft. 8½ in., depth 11 ft. 1 in. There is, none the less, a certain elephantine grandeur about it, and the reader can see for himself in the photographs that the carving is well up to the standard of the times. All the available evidence goes to show that, whereas in the past, the beds in great houses had been very simple affairs indeed with the woodwork almost wholly concealed by hangings, by the second half of the 16th century, though hangings were still essential and decidedly costly, great attention was paid to the actual bed structure. The Great Bed of Ware is exceptional, not on account of its elaborate carving, but merely because of its size. There were of course plenty of simple wooden beds for ordinary folk without foot-posts or ceiling, but it is clear that as soon as a man began to accumulate wealth and to rise in the social scale his first thought would be to order a bed which would bear witness to his importance by its solidity and by the richness of its carving ; and next perhaps to acquire a court cupboard on which to display his plate. Arcaded decoration and pilasters frequently adorned the head board just as they did the chimney piece, while posts and tester afforded excellent opportunities for the carver.

It is perhaps worth noting at this point that while new-fangled fashions in furniture began with the court and made their way downwards in the social hierarchy, there was no rapid change in the furnishings of the average prosperous household. Most people would cling to the ancient ways for lengthy periods and would be content to make use of the furniture they had inherited. However cumbersome the Elizabethan bed—and even when half the size of the Great Bed of Ware, it was cumbersome enough—there is little doubt that many were still in use a century later. The evidence of an occasional inventory affords sufficient proof of the strength of tradition. One, frequently quoted, is that which was made of the contents of the house near Devizes to which Robert Nicholas, Chief Baron of the Exchequer during the Commonwealth, retired after the Restoration in 1660. The hall contained a long trestle table with a leather cover and a livery cupboard—pieces which could well have been found in similar country houses throughout the country a hundred years previously, while in the master's bedroom were two bedsteads with green hangings. The guest chamber contained two beds—one of them a low truckle bed on wheels which could be run under the large bed during the day.

23. The Canopy of the Great Bed of Ware.

23

24. One of the bed posts.

24

25. The Headboard, with the false date 1463, carved in the early 19th century.

26. Carved Headboard from another 16th century bed, with original colours of red, green, yellow and blue.

Mr. L. G. G. Ramsey

27 *Victoria & Albert Museum*

Chest of cypress wood. Italian, 16th century.

28 *The City Museum and Art Gallery, Birmingham*

Chestnut Table with tessellated top. 16th century. Aston Hall, Birmingham.

29 *S. W. Wolsey*

Large leather-covered Box covered with tooled leather. Red leather in the interior. Iron mounts with handles for carrying.

30  *Trinity College Chapel, Toronto*

30. Oak Chair with linenfold panels. English, 16th century.

31 *Victoria & Albert Museum*

Carved oak Cupboard. Northern French, late 15th century.

32 *S. W. Wolsey*

Oak Chest. English, early 16th century. Wood pin hinges. All panels tongued.

33 & 34. Carved walnut Cabinet. Spanish, 16th century.

33 *Private Collection*

34 *Private Collection*

35 *Mr. R. T. Gwynn*

Carved oak Cupboard. English, late 16th century.

36. Oak Table with drawer leaves and carved bulbous supports. Late 16th century.

Mrs. Geoffrey Hart

37

Victoria & Albert Museum

Carved walnut Cabinet. Spanish, 16th century.

38 *The Victoria Wine Co.*

Oak Chair, inlay decoration. English, late 16th century.

39 *Victoria & Albert Museum*

Carved and painted oak. English, 16th century. Inscription and coat of arms added in the 19th century.

40 *S. W. Wolsey*

Oak Stool, with four sturdy bulbous carved legs. English, late 16th century.

41 *Mrs. Geoffrey Hart*

Small folding-top Games Table of oak. English, late 16th century.

42

The Dean and Chapter, Exeter Cathedral. Photo: courtesy of S. W. Wolsey

English Chair, late 16th century. The frame decorated in green, gold, cream, with trails of flowers. Part of the original green cut velvet intact.

43
Nonesuch Chest. Late 16th century.

44 *Victoria & Albert Museum*
Oak Chest. English, with ear supports. 16th century.

45 *Victoria & Albert Museum*
Oak Chest. English, with linenfold panelling. 16th century.

46 *Mrs. Geoffrey Hart*

Oak Press. Cupboard ornamented with turning, carving and inlay. English, late 16th century.

47 *Mallett & Son*

Oak Buffet or Cupboard. English, 16th century.

48 *Victoria & Albert Museum*

Chair of carved chestnut. Venetian, about 1560.

49 *S. W. Wolsey*

Carved oak Chair. English, of about the same date as Figure 48. Geometrical pattern inlay.

50 *S. W. Wolsey*

Oak Chair with carved and arcaded back.

51 *Victoria & Albert Museum*

Carved walnut X Chair. Italian, about 1550.

Victoria & Albert Museum

Walnut Cabinet, with inlay of various woods and coloured bone. Spanish, late 16th century.

53 *Victoria & Albert Museum*

Carved oak Cabinet. French, about 1560.

54 *Mr. R. T. Gwynn*

Oak close Chair. Pentagonal and undecorated. English, early 16th century.

55 *Victoria & Albert Museum*

Oak Chair. French, late 16th century.

56 *Mr. R. T. Gwynn*

Oak Counter or Rent Table. English, early 16th century.

The Seventeenth Century

FROM OAK TO WALNUT

If it is possible to sum up the course of furniture development during the reigns of James I and Charles I, one can say perhaps that the old forms—the court cupboard, the table, the bench—remained, but less lavishly carved and of a plainer design. It is almost as if the troubles of the middle of the century were casting their shadows before them and ham-stringing inventiveness. Oak remained the normal material. Chests with drawers were mentioned in inventories as early as the 16th century, but the earliest recorded example of the complete chest of drawers dates from the mid 17th. Joined panelled chairs have survived in considerable numbers, supported on baluster legs joined by stretchers, but we possibly credit the more prosperous subjects of Charles I, as indeed of Elizabeth I, with greater hardihood than they would claim for themselves because, although uncommonly few have survived, upholstered chairs were in existence. In such things naturally the quality of the wood is unimportant. In an X frame chair for example, the wood—beech or other soft wood—would be covered with fabric, velvet perhaps, trimmed with fringed galons and studded with brass-headed nails. Folding chairs of this character were known in Italy, France, and Tudor England, and were still being made in the 17th century, but as their value depended entirely upon their perishable covering it is not surprising that they are rarely seen. A famous set of upholstered chairs at Knole, Sevenoaks, is a notable survival. To what extent the more delicate furniture suffered damage during the troubles of the civil war is not known ; it may have been considerable for it seems likely that many householders must have had similar experiences to those of Dame Mary Verney who, returning to Claydon after four years absence wrote : " I feare they will make us very poore as beggers ; I protest I know nott which way we shall live if the countrey may allwayes quarter soldiers." The house was " most lamentably furnished, all the linnen quite worne out . . . . . the spitts, and other odd things so extreamely eaten with Rust that they cannot be of any use againe . . . . the cloath of the Musk-coloured stools spoyled, and the dining-room chairs in Ragges."

The Restoration of Charles II in 1660 marked the beginning of a new age in which furniture became more complicated and more luxurious and the cabinetmaker, as we understand the term, gradually took the place of the joiner. Oak and the other woods—elm, yew, beech—continued to be used for less pretentious pieces, but the fashionable wood was walnut, supplied partly from native sources and partly by importations from France and to a lesser degree from Virginia. Both Holland and France influenced design, though we never achieved either the monumental dignity or the luxury of the furniture made by Boulle and his contemporaries for the French court. The solid Derbyshire and Yorkshire chairs in oak have survived in considerable numbers and the earliest recorded bookcases, made in oak for Samuel Pepys in the summer of 1666 by " Sympson the Joyner " are to be seen in the Pepys Library at Magdalene College, Cambridge, together with the Diarist's writing desk (Fig. 95). It is remarkable that no such thing as a table set aside specifically for writing appears to have been owned by Charles I, as cultured a prince as any in Christendom. Upholstered winged armchairs were first introduced at this period ; one from Ham House is illustrated in Fig. 89. Marquetry soon became modish, generally an intricate pattern of flowers or arabesques made by gluing on thin strips of veneer as distinct from the older and clumsier method of inlay, which involved the insertion of pieces of wood or ivory or bone into the solid. A very pleasant refinement is the use of the so-called oyster veneer—that is, a section of the walnut obtained by cutting obliquely across the grain of the smaller branches. Whole cabinets and the cases of clocks are extremely effective when treated in this manner. For pieces made in the solid the wood was straight cut—that is cut with, not across, the grain. The other woods in general use as subsidiary foils to the main design of the walnut veneers were laburnum, cedar, olive and kingwood. Chairs were of walnut, the cheaper varieties of beech, with both backs and seats of caning, replacing fabric or leather. Legs and stretchers were turned. Later, rails and cresting were carved and also the front stretcher, and the arms have scrolled ends. Towards the end of the century backs become much higher with an arched top. The heavy oak draw-tables of a past fashion were still made in the country, but the circular or oval gate-legged table, sometimes of oak, more rarely of walnut, made its appearance. Cane chairs continued to be made long after they had fallen out of favour with the leaders of society; even as late as about 1740 one could go to St. Paul's Churchyard and buy a cane chair with carved walnut frame for 10/- or 15/- and a beech chair for 5/-. In the last years of the century a chair based on French and Italian models, described as "in the style of Daniel Marot," the Huguenot who was Minister of Works to William of Orange, was introduced. It was a chair with a narrow, slightly carved back and cabriole legs, with scroll or hoof feet—the club and the claw and ball foot were destined to follow ten or fifteen years later towards the close of the reign of Queen Anne. To see a great house of the time of Charles II more or less as it was when it was originally furnished one must visit Ham House. The place had been altered and fitted up in what was then the most modern manner by James Duke of Lauderdale and his managing Duchess in the years 1673–75 and was immediately famous. Evelyn walked over to see it one summer's day in 1678 and noted that it was "indeede inferior to few of the best villas in Italy itselfe, the house furnished like a great Prince's." The diarist's own tastes were simpler, for elsewhere he deplored our "more than Asiatick luxury." Chests of drawers—a natural development from the chest or coffer—were sometimes placed on stands of yew or chestnut; the transition from this to the tallboy of the early 18th century is obvious enough. The finer cabinets would be enclosed by solid doors and contain numerous small drawers grouped round a central cupboard. One or two small walnut writing-tables have survived from about the 1670's, but the large bureaux standing on chests of drawers, with drop fronts disclosing pigeon holes do not appear to have been made before about 1690. In general, little movable box-like desks would be used for writing materials and placed on an ordinary table—these exist both in walnut and oak. Less pretentious households would have solidly made oak cupboards and oak dressers, decorated with less ornate carving than that customary a century earlier but none the less springing from the older tradition. When communications are slow and difficult, remote regions cling to the ancient ways and pay little attention to what, in their view, are merely the modish fads of court circles, and the same holds true of most countries.

While this not inconsiderable revolution in taste was going on in England in our usual haphazard manner, things were happening in France. Our own craftsmen owed much to France and Holland, France in her turn to Italy. But while we learnt the skills of the Continent aided by decidedly casual Government patronage, Colbert, Louis XIV's brilliant Minister, made of his newly-founded academy and of its subsidiary "La Manufacture Royale des Meubles de la Couronne" the centre and mainspring of a deliberately planned scheme to promote the arts in the widest sense of the word—to bring under a centralised direction not merely what are known as the fine arts, but also their humbler partners among which the craft of the cabinetmaker is not the least. The royal letters patent of the years 1662 and 1667 lay down that the Superintendent and the Director of this organisation shall "fill the house" (i.e. L'Hôtel des Gobelins) "with good painters, tapestry workers, silversmiths, founders, engravers, lapidaries, wood workers and other good workmen in every kind of art and craft." Colbert's object was not merely to control the style and decoration of the royal palaces; it was to find a means to foster in France and among Frenchmen those special skills which up till then had been largely in the hands of foreigners. Many of the workpeople were Italian, and the Director himself, Charles Le Brun, was a painter steeped in the tradition of Italian painting; in spite of that, and also because Le Brun was clearly a man able to organise a team, there came out of this somewhat ponderous official scheme, something which was a distinctly French style, owing much to Italy it is true, but influencing all Europe in its turn—a style luxurious and majestic which was, in the 18th century, and in the hands of a few exceptional cabinetmakers, to produce some of the most delicately civilised pieces yet known to man. One great name among numerous gifted designers and makers—that of Charles André Boulle—is specially memorable, not because in the course of his long life his reputation had become almost legendary (he lived to be 90) or because his type of furniture was imitated *ad nauseam* during the 19th century, but because the magnificent pieces made by him for Versailles—Palace Furniture in the most literal sense of the word—set a standard of craftsmanship for the furniture trade which did much to ensure its reputation in the years to come. Boulle was born in 1642, the son of the King's cabinetmaker; by the time he was thirty his abilities as bronze-chaser and worker in metals, and as engraver and as cabinetmaker were fully recognised. He it was who can be said to have first led the way in the marriage of gilded bronze (ormolu) and woodwork—not by any means to everyone's taste today—and to have brought to an extraordinary degree of perfection the technique of marquetry in tortoiseshell, pewter, bone, mother-of-pearl, ivory and brass upon a foundation of wood. Typical Boulle workmanship is illustrated in Figs. 94 and 97—the latter is a particularly fine example, while the earlier type of marquetry of the reign of Louis XIII is seen in Fig. 96. Boulle, in addition to his renown as the greatest cabinetmaker of the long reign of Louis XIV was also an impassioned collector of works of art. All these were lost in a fire in 1720 together with many of his own productions.

57 *Sotheby's*

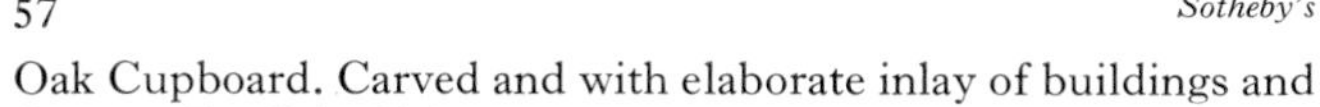

Oak Cupboard. Carved and with elaborate inlay of buildings and flowers. English, 16th century.

58 *Christchurch Mansion, Ipswich*

Oak Cupboard, simple geometrical inlay. English, 17th century.

59 *S. W. Wolsey*

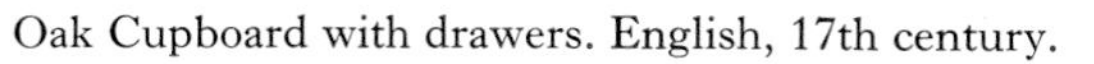

Oak Cupboard with drawers. English, 17th century.

60 *Christchurch Mansion, Ipswich*

Oak Dresser, with door panels decorated with floral inlay. English, 17th century.

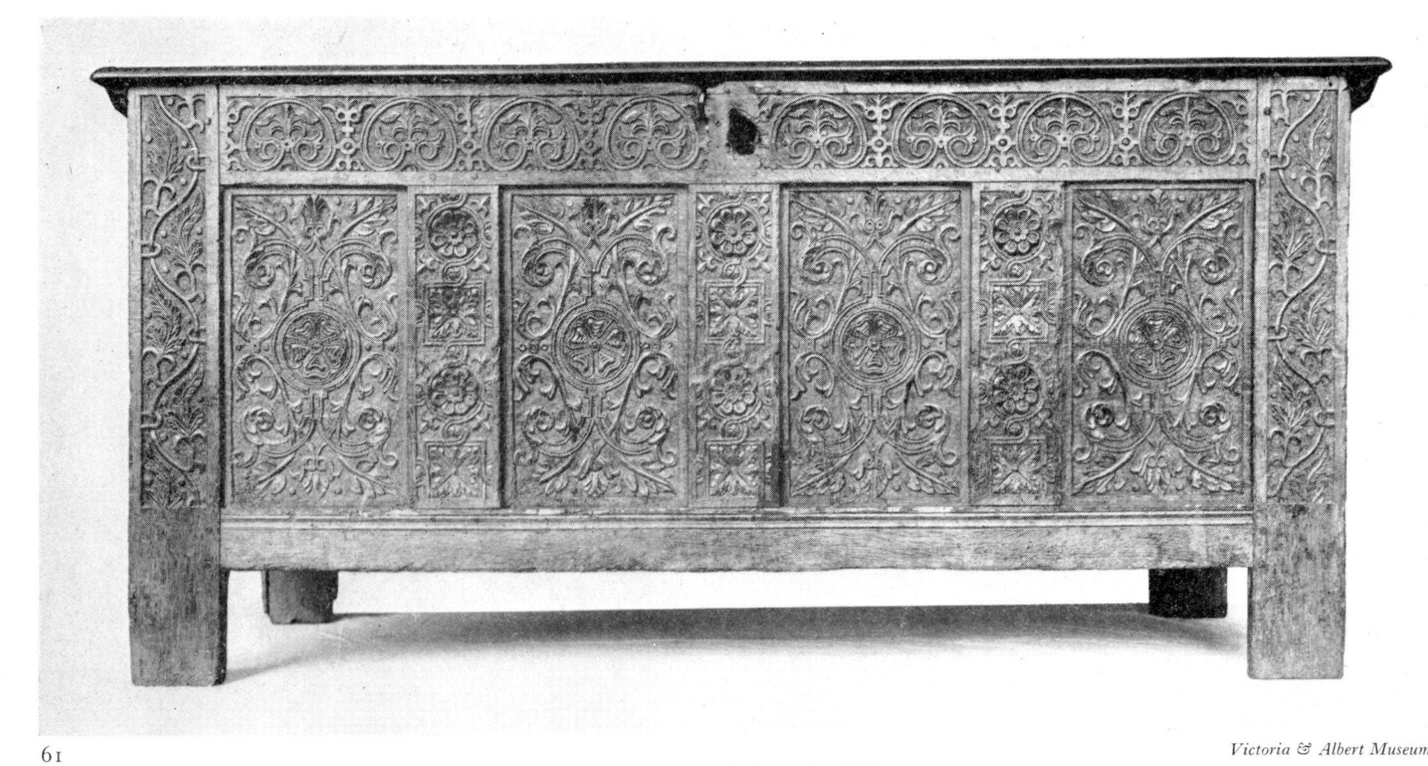

61 *Victoria & Albert Museum*

Carved oak Chest. English, early 17th century.

62 *Victoria & Albert Museum*

Oak Chair of the so-called "Glastonbury" type. English, 17th century. A style greatly admired by 19th century ecclesiastical furnishers.

63 *Victoria & Albert Musuem*

Carved walnut Chair. Italian, 17th century.

64 *Victoria & Albert Museum*

64. Walnut Chair. Spanish, 17th century; the velvet cover of a later date.

65. Cedarwood Cabinet. Portuguese, 17th century. Probably made in GOA, India.

65 *Victoria & Albert Museum*

66 *Victoria & Albert Museum*

Walnut Chair. Italian, 17th century.

67 *Victoria & Albert Museum*

Oak so-called "Farthingale" Chair. English, 17th century.

68 *Mr. Alfred Jowett*

Walnut writing Bureau. English, about 1670. The ancestor of a long series of ingenious walnut and mahogany pieces.

69 *Mrs. Geoffrey Hart*

Walnut writing Bureau. English, about 1690.

Victoria & Albert Museum

Oak Bookcase. English, about 1670.

71 *Victoria & Albert Museum*

Chair of turned walnut, caned back and seat. An early type, probably made in considerable numbers, and now very rare. English, about 1660.

72 *M. Harris & Sons*

Carved walnut Chair. English, about 1675.

73 *Victoria & Albert Museum*

Carved walnut Chair. English, about 1675.

74 *Victoria & Albert Museum*

Carved walnut Chair. English, about 1675.

75. Louis XIV giltwood Stool. French, about 1690.

76. Carved walnut Chair. English, about 1690.

77. Carved and painted beechwood Chair. English, about 1690.

78. Carved walnut Chair. About 1690.

75 *Christie's*

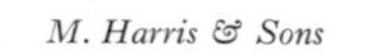

76 *M. Harris & Sons*

77 *Victoria & Albert Museum*

78 *Frank Partridge & Sons*

79 *Frank Partridge & Sons*

Walnut Table with floral marquetry turned legs, shaped stretcher and bun feet. About 1690.

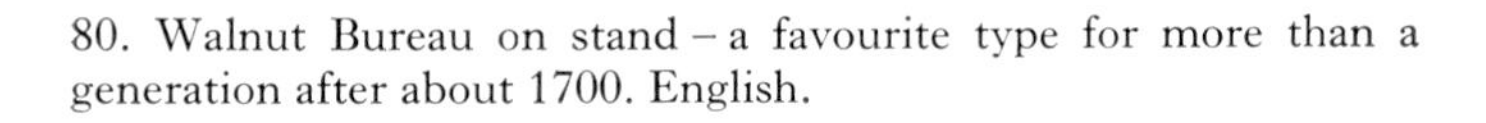

80. Walnut Bureau on stand – a favourite type for more than a generation after about 1700. English.

80 *Frank Partridge & Sons*

81 *S. W. Wolsey*

Simple walnut Daybed. English, about 1700.

82 *Frank Partridge & Sons*

A Settee of walnut inlaid with satinwood, covered in green brocatelle. Pointed pad feet. English, about 1700.

83 *Frank Partridge & Sons*

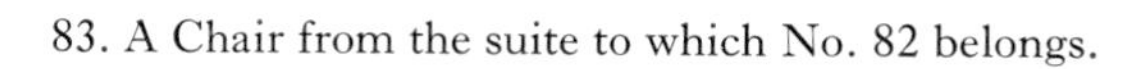

83. A Chair from the suite to which No. 82 belongs.

84 *Private Collection*

85 *Private Collection*

84 & 85. A rare walnut gate-leg Table, shut and open. English, about 1700.

86 *Hotspur Ltd.*

87 *Victoria & Albert Museum*

Chair and Stool of about 1695. Walnut. English.

86. High-back Chair, about 1700, covered in contemporary silk damask. English.

88 *Temple Newsam, Leeds*

Hall Seat carved in fruit wood. English, about 1690.

89. "Sleeping Chair" from Ham House. English, about 1670.

89 *Victoria & Albert Museum*

90 *Hotspur Ltd.*

91 *Frank Partridge & Sons*

Tall upright Mirror with carved gilded pediment, the side plates with carved gilded panels. English, about 1690.

90. Early 18th century English walnut long case Clock by Daniel Delander.

92. Long case walnut Clock, decorated with floral marquetry.

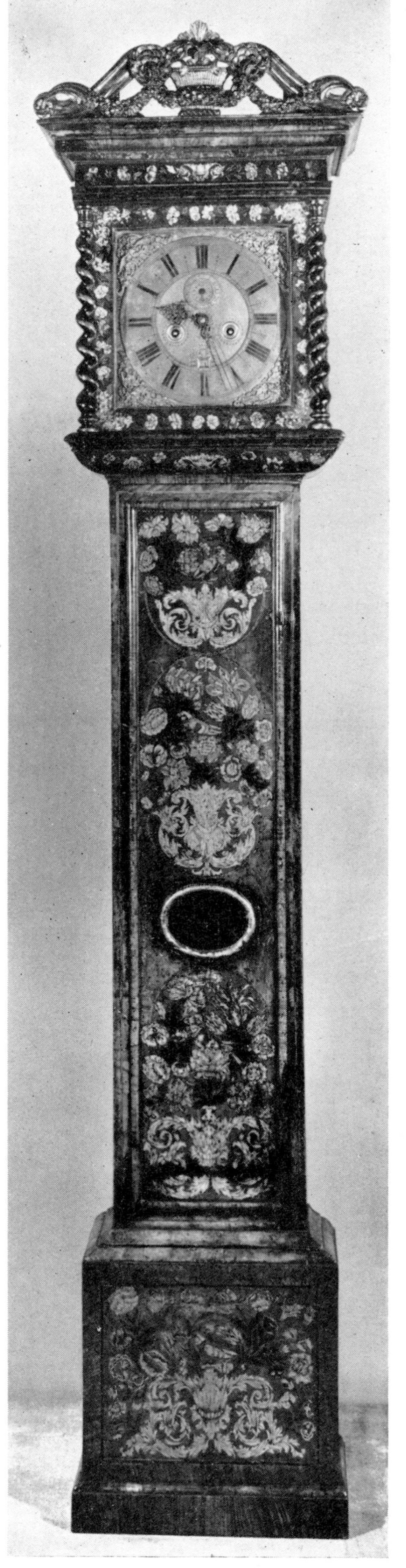

92 *Hotspur Ltd.*

93 *The Detroit Institute of Arts*

Carved ebony Cabinet on stand. Probably French, early 17th century.

94. Pedestal Table decorated with Boulle marquetry. French, Louis XIV.

Victoria & Albert Museum

95

The Master and Fellows of Magdalene College

Oak pedestal Writing Desk, made for Samuel Pepys. English, about 1680. In the Pepys Library at Magdalene College, Cambridge.

96. Cabinet decorated with marquetry of various woods and ivory. French, period of Louis XIII.

96

Victoria & Albert Museum

97

Victoria & Albert Museum

Armoire. French, probably designed by Berain and executed by Boulle for Louis XIV. The cypher of Louis XIV – the double L – on each of the doors.

Victoria & Albert Museum

Walnut Bureau decorated in marquetry of various woods. English, about 1700. Obvious Dutch influence.

99 *Private Collection*

99 & 100. Walnut gate-leg Table decorated in elaborate floral marquetry. English, about 1700.

100 *Private Collection*

101 *Mallett & Son*

Walnut gate-leg Table of the 1690's. English. The fold-over top encloses a small well with tray and secret drawers.

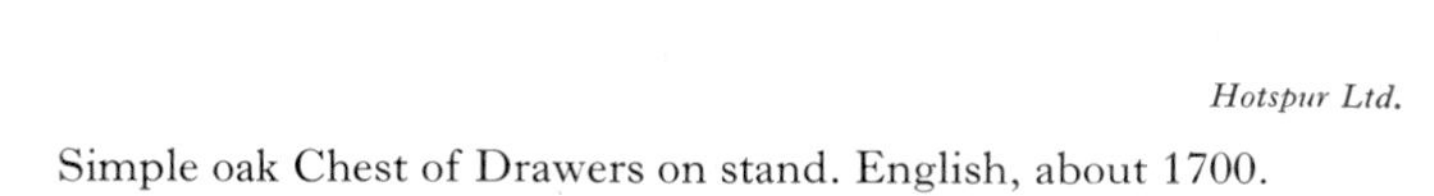

102 *Hotspur Ltd.*

Simple oak Chest of Drawers on stand. English, about 1700.

Chinese Furniture and Chinese Influence

It seems worth while to pause at this point, and say something about the way in which the art of the Far East stirred the imagination of Europe and exercised a very definite spell over furniture makers as well as over manufacturers of pottery and porcelain. Our ancestors—the majority of the stay-at-homes at any rate—had very vague notions of geography and were by no means certain about the identity of such different countries as China, Japan, and India. Indeed, Chinese lacquer screens are, to this day, known to everyone as Coromandel screens as if they were made on the Coromandel coast of India, when all that happened was that they were transhipped at that convenient halfway house from Chinese or Arab vessels to the East India Company's ships and so came to Europe. While a few—a very few—pieces of Chinese porcelain had reached Europe by the 16th century, much lacquer, silks and other goods were pouring into Portugal, Holland and France by the middle of the 17th century, so that, with the Restoration of Charles II in 1660, and the introduction of a more luxurious standard of furnishing, the popularity of the highly decorative Chinese and Japanese lacquers was assured in England as it was already on the continent. But it is necessary to add that throughout the next two centuries and later, most Europeans were more impressed by the strangeness and glamour of the Far East than by its less colourful characteristics. They would almost certainly have rejected such a table as that shown in Fig. 103 as of no commercial or aesthetic interest—whereas it is not only wholly Chinese but a wonderful example of simple, lucid design, with a lacquer covering of incomparable quality. It has to be remembered that in those days none of us knew anything whatever about China and that our contacts with the mysterious yellow men were left largely to the sea captains who, though good companions in a scrap, were scarcely competent to form a judgment in matters of this sort. In any case the more obviously gorgeous pieces were to the taste of the market. Lacquer was the rage quite soon after the Restoration and was speedily imitated. Two enthusiasts, Stalker and Parker, published in 1688 a pamphlet entitled *Treatise on Japanning and Varnishing* in which amateurs were instructed how to proceed and in which occur flights of fancy unusual in practical How-to-do-it Books. Few of us could easily resist this: "What can be more surprising than to have our Chambers overlaid with Varnish more glossy and reflecting than polished Marble? No amorous Nymph need entertain a dialogue with her glass, or Narcissus retire to a Fountain to survey his charming countenance when the whole house is one entire speculum. . . ." From now until the end of the 18th century importations continued more or less steadily. Lacquer cabinets—either red and gold or black and gold—were specially favoured and would be provided with specially made stands in gilt or silver gilt, elaborately carved and as unoriental as it is possible to imagine. Later—and particularly after the turn of the century—chairs and writing bureaux and toilet mirrors and long case clocks would be painted in the Chinese manner, the forms remaining typically early 18th century, while, in the 1750's, fashion demanded a gay legion of wall mirrors, with gilded frames carved with all kinds of pseudo-oriental devices—the type of design associated with the name of Thomas Chippendale. It is of interest to note that some of the best pieces of imitation Oriental lacquer made in England have been found in Spain and Portugal; there was evidently a considerable export trade to both countries in the 1730's and 40's. The illustrations which are grouped together in this section provide, I hope, a reasonably balanced view of both Oriental styles and of what Europeans made of them. Other imitation Chinese pieces will be found side by side with the normal production of the English and French cabinetmakers on other pages. The French made particularly careful use of imported panels for the sides of cabinets, and the fashion for a judicious use of lacquer—whether imported or Paris made—lasted right up to the revolution of 1789. With us the influence of Robert Adam was sufficient, by about 1770, to put an end to the Chinese craze, until it was revived again after 1800, as can still be seen in the furniture made for the Royal Pavilion at Brighton. At this distance of time we are able to smile at the gay extravagancies of some of the mid-18th century productions, which, with our more exact knowledge of Chinese design, we can see easily enough bear only a superficial resemblance to the real thing. At the same time, such an ingenious flight of fancy as the famous bed from Badminton, though perhaps few of us would care to sleep in it, is surely more than a mere whimsy; it is finely proportioned and by no means without dignity. Then there are the mahogany chairs with their lattice work backs and with small pagoda-like roofs instead of cresting; they must have been produced in considerable quantities. These are among the most sober and elegant productions of their day, but none the less in essence un-Chinese. It is a mark of the continued popularity of this mongrel style that while Messrs. Stalker and Parker issued their little book of instructions in 1688, similar instructions were published in 1760 in *The Ladies Amusement or Whole Art of Japanning*, in which the readers are warned that if the scene is European they should not place in it any "exotic or preposterous object." On the other hand "with Indian or Chinese greater liberties may be taken—for in these is often seen a butterfly supporting an elephant or things equally absurd." In short, we persisted in looking upon the Chinese as "quaint," instead of as the inheritors of a superb and essentially austere artistic tradition. The result is that to the average Westerner, accustomed to the changing styles of our own furniture evolution, the rare pieces of authentic Chinese furniture he sees appear disconcertingly modern in their simplicity, when in fact they merely embody principles at least two thousand years old. Nails were never used and the whole piece would be put together by skilful joining. Favourite woods were the various types of rosewood, sandalwood and the so-called red wood rather like mahogany.

We commonly refer rather glibly to lacquer and as a rule forget the great difference there is between the Far Eastern variety and the European imitation of it. The Chinese—and the Japanese learnt the technique from them—obtained their effects by laying on successive thin coats of the sap of the *Rhus Vernicifera*, a lengthy and laborious process requiring infinite patience. For flat lacquer with painted decoration the wood foundation would be smoothed to perfection, paper or linen or silk placed on it, sized and polished, and then layer after layer of lac applied; each coat dried and polished in turn. Only then would the design be drawn and the colours filled in. The technique for the other type of lacquer work—carved lacquer, as in the throne of the Emperor illustrated in Fig. 3, was yet more laborious. Here the lacquer was built up to the required richness and then carved—a difficult process in any event and infinitely more difficult when layers of different colours were used and the carver obtained the desired result by cutting down to expose whatever colour was required at a particular point. It is scarcely necessary to add that such work was never attempted—nor for that matter imagined—in Europe, or that such elaborate ceremonial chairs as the one illustrated were commonplace. Not unnaturally when the demands of the export trade became insistent, such high standards were liable to be disregarded; for example, to save

John Sparks

Table of creamy-white lacquer with high cross stretchers. Chinese. Ming Dynasty (A.D. 1368-1644).

time, wood would be carved and then coated with lacquer. The result is pleasant enough, but lacks the extraordinary refinement of the best work.

In contrast to this highly skilled craft, the European imitations, often agreeable, sometimes distinguished, were no more than painting in gum-copal. In England the craze lasted from the early years of Charles II until about 1720. After that it seems to have been largely confined to clock-cases for a few years. Then, as has already been noted, came the more than oriental fantasies of the 1750's, and a certain revival of interest after 1800.

In China, for more modest households, bamboo was cheap, comely and serviceable—and this also was imitated occasionally by Chippendale and his contemporaries. Nevertheless the fact remains that in neither England, nor Holland, nor France was there any genuine understanding until our own times of the extraordinary contribution China, and to a lesser degree Japan, had made to the arts at a time when our own ancestors had been running about the forests painted with woad. And of all those contributions, furniture is what we know least; the best of it was too severe, too traditional, too much the reverse of "quaint" to please us at that time. Not even the sober splendour of the lacquered chest of Fig. 106 or the beautifully made bride's chest of drawers of Fig. 115 would have been showy enough.

104 *Sotheby's*

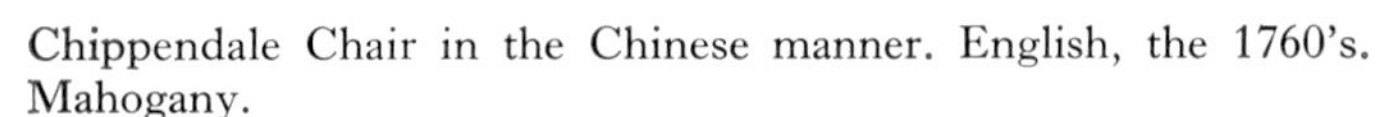

Chippendale Chair in the Chinese manner. English, the 1760's. Mahogany.

105 *Spink & Sons*

Rosewood Chair. Chinese, 18th century.

106 *Bluett & Sons*

Chest of brown lacquer, the design in orange-yellow, slightly raised and picked out with gold. Chinese, 17th century.

107 *Spink & Sons*

Rosewood Table, with an openwork frieze of rectangular and scroll designs. Chinese, 19th century.

108 *Christie's*

Typical so-called Coromandel Screen. Chinese, about 1700. Each leaf 9 ft. 4 in. high.

109 *Frank Partridge & Sons*

110 *Frank Partridge & Sons*

109. Walnut Bureau with painted decoration in the Chinese manner. English, by Hugh Grainger; early 18th century.

110. The Bureau open.

111 *Frank Partridge & Sons*

112 *Frank Partridge & Sons*

111 & 112. Details of the decoration of Nos. 109-110.

113 *Frank Partridge & Sons*

Chinoiserie wall Mirror. French, about 1700.

114 *Frank Partridge & Sons*

Painted Commode decorated with Sevres porcelain plaques. French, late 18th century. Chinese influence with a French accent.

115 *H. J. Hewett Ltd.*

Marriage Chest. 6 ft. 3 in. in height. Brown and gold lacquer. Chinese, 17th century.

116 *Victoria & Albert Museum*

116. Bed in carved and gilt lacquer. Chinese.

117 *Spink & Sons*

117. Rosewood Cabinet, carved with archaic bronze designs; gilt metal fittings. Chinese, late 18th century.

118 & 119 *Victoria & Albert Museum*

Lacquer Cabinet. Chinese, 18th century; and below, the cabinet open.

120 *Mr. Victor Kaye*

121 *Mr. Victor Kaye*

Cabinet of pale brown wood enriched with applique decoration in finely carved and vari-coloured soapstones. The gilded bronze mounts engraved with floral motifs. Chinese, 18th century; and above, cabinet open (120).

122 *Victoria & Albert Museum*

Lacquered and gilt Bedstead from Badminton. English, about 1760.

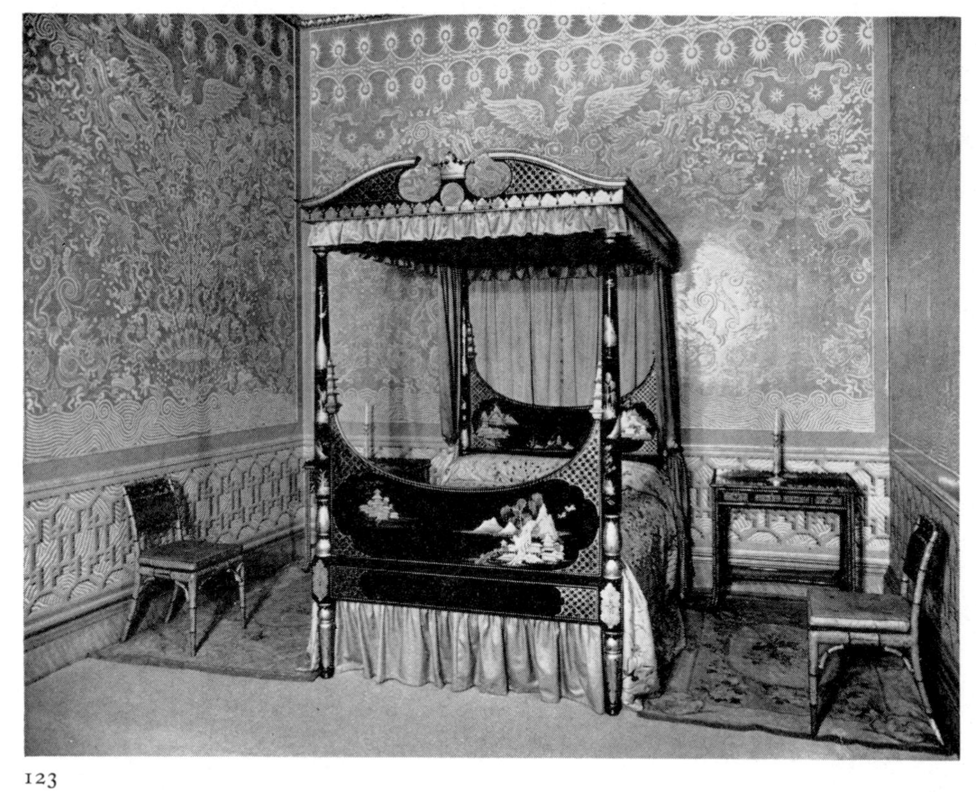

123

The Bed Recess of the King's bedroom at the Brighton Pavilion. The furniture made by Edward Marsh and Tatham in 1802.

124 *Christie's*

Small gilt carved Mirror in the Chinese manner; English, attributable to Thomas Johnson. Mid 18th century.

125 *Christchurch Mansion, Ipswich*

Chest of Drawers; painted wood imitating Chinese lacquer; English, about 1710.

126 *Victoria & Albert Museum*

Japanned wood Cabinet. English, mid 18th century.

127 *Hotspur Ltd.*

Walnut Settee with "flying" brackets. English, early 18th century.

Walnut to Mahogany

QUEEN ANNE TO CHIPPENDALE

The accession of Queen Anne in 1702 witnessed a gradual return to a more simple style, the normal swing of fashion from the exuberant to the sober. A similar trend is to be seen in other crafts, notably in silver. Instead of the elaboration of the last part of the 17th century the finer pieces are composed of carefully matched walnut veneers of superb quality. Gesso, already noticed as introduced about 1690, two hundred years after it was a commonplace in Florence, continues in favour for particularly choice tables for another 30 years or so. The cabriole leg, which came across the Channel in a singularly graceful form in the train of William III, now becomes established as the normal chair leg for the next half century and more. Perhaps two types of chair can be considered customary at this period—first, the one with a plain walnut spoon-shaped back, and then the type with a square stuffed back. These were the standard patterns for a quarter of a century, differing mainly in the quality of the carving (or lack of it) on the knee and in the shape of the foot—chiefly the club foot, soon to be the claw and ball. The carving on the latter can be revealing—in some early chairs the claw and ball seem thoroughly perfunctory performances, in others the claw will grip the ball in a convincing manner. No doubt mahogany would have gained popular favour in any case; it is a beautiful wood, but it's more general adoption in England was hastened by a wholly fortuitous circumstance—an exceptionally severe winter which resulted in a walnut tree famine in France and an embargo on export. This threw the London trade into considerable difficulties, and, though the price was high, mahogany from San Domingo and Cuba was the answer. Moreover, while it was not suitable as veneer, it was closer grained and withstood the attacks of wood worm much better than walnut. We probably have a false notion of the relative amount of furniture produced in the two woods from about 1720 until 1730 or 40 for this very reason; far more walnut has disappeared. At first chairs of identical design would be made in either wood and stretchers, unnecessary with the strong cabriole leg (and moreover unsightly in combination with it), disappeared for a generation. Mahogany lent itself admirably to the knife of the carver and the chairs and other pieces—side tables for example—of this early mahogany decade can show some remarkably crisp and vigorous examples of his skill—the carved eagle's head of an arm terminal, or the shell or acanthus foliage on a chair knee. Today we are accustomed to the dark reddish-brown colour of 18th century mahogany pieces, mellowed by the polishings of two hundred years. It is perhaps worth reminding ourselves that there is evidence enough to show that our ancestors appreciated a far brighter red, that in the country joiners are said to have stained oak with bullock's blood; certainly in the majority of paintings of the interiors of the time the furniture appears to be of a warmer red than we see today. In France the delicate grandeur of the style which had been evolved to glorify the power of the monarchy began to lose something of its solemnity towards the end of the reign of Louis XIV (he died in 1715). Imperceptibly almost it became more gracious, more subtly curved, a change which can be seen especially in the fine commodes of the first twenty-five years of the 18th century—a style known inaccurately as Régence—with their flowing curves and beautifully chiselled ormolu handles and escutcheons; a type of furniture which has been appreciated in England only recently. Charles André Boulle—the great Boulle—was still active and soon his two sons were to carry on his very special techniques. His influence was perhaps important in preventing his pupils, successors and imitators from passing the bounds of good sense. But the real interest of these early years of the century in France lies in the fact that now began that tradition of singularly graceful design reinforced by the most precise control of ormolu and marquetry which renders the work of the great French cabinet-makers of the next two generations so consistently memorable. The use of metal for marquetry in the manner of Boulle was gradually discarded—it was scarcely ever attempted in England; instead many woods, exotic and native, were pressed into service to produce the flowing floral marquetry or the more formal arabesques or trophies or musical instruments which are among the most attractive enrichments of French furniture throughout the century.

128 *Sotheby's*

Walnut Settee. English, early 18th century.

129 *Mallett & Son*

129. Mirror, in simple walnut frame. English, early 18th century.

130 *Sotheby's*

130. Dressing-table Mirror decorated in gilt and white chinoiseries on a vermilion ground. English, early 18th century type.

131 *Williamson & Sons*

Wing Armchair of about 1720. English.

132 *Sotheby's*

Small walnut Settee. English, early 18th century.

133 *Private Collection*

Walnut Chair, with carved knees, pad feet, stuffed seat and back. English, about 1710.

134 *Parke-Bernet Galleries, New York*

Mahogany Stool. English, probably about 1730.

135 *Christie's*

Walnut and gesso Stool. English, probably about 1720.

136 *Frank Partridge & Sons*

Pedestal writing Bureau of figured walnut. English. First years of the 18th century or earlier.

137 *Christie's*

Walnut writing Bureau, with three drawers slightly "set back" one above the other. English, early 18th century.

138 *Christie's*

Walnut writing Bureau. English, early 18th century, with stretchers in the 17th century tradition.

139 *Mallett & Son*

Walnut writing Bureau of the finest quality, shown open. English, early 18th century.

140. Mirror in carved gilt frame. Two candle brackets. English, about 1730.

141. Walnut Chair. English, early 18th century.

142. Mirror in carved and gilt gesso. English, early 18th century.

143. Chair in carved and gilded walnut. English, early 18th century.

140 *Knight, Frank & Rutley*

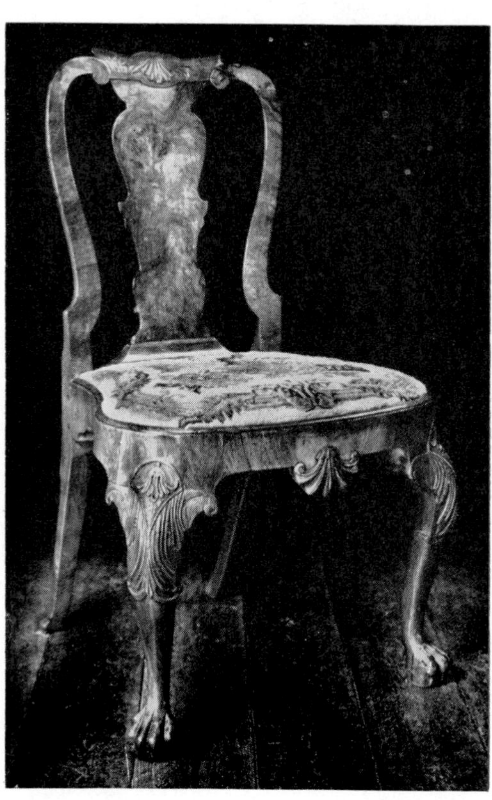

141 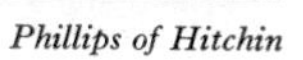 *Phillips of Hitchin*

142 *Christie's*

143 *Mallett & Son*

144 *Christie's*

Mahogany Chair. Dutch, early 18th century.

145 *Christie's*

Walnut Chair. English, early 18th century. Typical "Queen Anne" type.

146 *Sotheby's*

X-frame Chair, painted in black and gold on a japanned red ground. Covered in red cut-silk velvet. English ? early 18th century.

147 *Christchurch Mansion, Ipswich*

Chair, carved and gilt, silk covered. William Kent design. English, about 1730.

148. Small walnut Settee, claw and ball feet, hoof foot at back. English, about 1725.

149. Chair, walnut, open back, flower heads carved at each end of top rail, flower carved cabriole legs, lion's claw and ball feet. English, about 1725.

150. Chair, the frame of turned and painted beech, upholstered in Soho tapestry. English, early 18th century.

148 *M. Harris & Sons*

149 *Frank Partridge & Sons*

150 *Victoria & Albert Museum*

151 *Mallett & Son*

Carved breakfront Bookcase of pinewood with cupboards below. Style of William Kent. English, about 1740.

152 *Victoria & Albert Museum*

Chest of wood, covered with embroidery on turned stand. Probably Dutch, about 1700.

153 *Christchurch Mansion, Ipswich*

Walnut drop-front Secretaire-cabinet. English, early 18th century.

154 *Victoria & Albert Museum*

Walnut Cabinet on stand. Superb use of walnut veneers. English, early 18th century.

155. Walnut Secretaire-cabinet. English, early 18th century. Dutch influence.

155 *Christie's*

156 *Victoria & Albert Museum*

Walnut Chest. English, about 1710.

157 *Christie's*

Commode in kingwood, mounted in ormolu. Stamped J. F. Lapie. French, about 1730.

158 *Victoria & Albert Museum*

158. Library Chair. English, about 1740. One sits astride facing the reading desk, resting one's elbows on the arms and warming one's back at the fire. Absurdly and falsely described in some quarters as a "cock-fighting chair."

159

Walnut Chair, slightly gilded. Acanthus leaf and scroll carving. Scroll and foliage feet. English, about 1725.

160 *Christie's*

Side Table in gilt gesso, the knees carved with foliage in low relief. English, early 18th century. (The marble top a later addition.)

161 *Christie's*

Carved side Table. Mahogany, in the style of William Kent. English, about 1735.

162. Mahogany Bookcase, possibly by William Vile. English, mid-18th century.

162 *Christie's*

163 *Mr. L. G. G. Ramsey*

164 *Mrs. Geoffrey Hart*

Card Table in walnut, of a type more usually found in mahogany. English, mid-18th century.

163. Mahogany Bookcase. English, mid-18th century.

165 *Victoria & Albert Museum*

Carved mahogany Chest, copied from the Medici sarcophagus in Florence. English, about 1740.

166 *Frank Partridge & Sons*

Carved and gilt Mirror. English, about 1740.

167 *Mrs. Geoffrey Hart*

Mahogany Table on a tripod base. The top has a pie-crust edge. English, about 1745.

168 *Hotspur Ltd.*

Mirror with gilt enrichments. English, early 18th century.

169 *Christie's*

Walnut Bureau-cabinet. Two bevelled mirror doors. The two centre columns surmounted by metal-gilt foliage, capitals with figures of Mercury and a Muse. English, early 18th century.

170 *Frank Partridge & Sons*

Card Table, walnut. English, early 18th century.

171 *Quinneys Ltd.*

Card Table, walnut. English, early 18th century.

172 *Sotheby's*

Walnut Bureau-cabinet. English, early 18th century.

173 *Parke-Bernet Galleries, New York*

Commode in mahogany, by J. M. Chevallier, with ormolu mounts. French, mid-18th century.

174 *Temple Newsam, Leeds*

Bureau-cabinet, mahogany. English, about 1735. An early example of the use of fine mahogany on this scale.

175 *Biggs & Co.*

Bureau-cabinet decorated with flowers painted on a black ground. English, early 18th century.

176 *Mallett & Son*

Chest of Drawers in finely figured walnut. English, early 18th century.

177

The Kitchen at the Governor's Palace, Williamsburg, Virginia, furnished with pewter, copper, brass and iron utensils of the 18th century.

178 *Biggs & Co.*

Cabinet with mirrored doors and painted with flowers in colours on a black ground. English, early 18th century.

179 *Frank Partridge & Sons*

Gilt landscape Mirror, with its three original mirror plates. English, early 18th century.

180 *Hotspur Ltd.*

Walnut marquetry Bureau-cabinet. English, early 18th century.

181 & 182 *Hotspur Ltd.*

Unusual mahogany adjustable Table. English, about 1740.

183 *Victoria & Albert Museum*

Carved mahogany side Table. Style of William Kent.

184 *Christchurch Mansion, Ipswich*

Writing Bureau of painted wood. English, early 18th century.

185 *Mrs. Geoffrey Hart*

Mirror with gilt gesso frame carved in low relief. English, about 1710.

186 *Hotspur Ltd.*

Walnut Chair. English, early 18th century.

187 *Frank Partridge & Sons*

Walnut Chair covered in Mortlake tapestry, the knees carved with shells. Pad feet. English, about 1710.

188 *Needhams, New York*

Carved walnut Chair. All four legs carved with foliage; lion's paw feet. English, about 1740.

189 *Christchurch Mansion, Ipswich*

Chair and Stool. Walnut. English, about 1710.

190 *Hotspur Ltd.*

Carved and gilt Sidetable with marble top, perhaps by Benjamin Goodison. About 1735.

191 *Christie's*

Walnut and gilt Sidetable, the top inlaid with arrow pattern bands. English, early 18th century.

192 *Sotheby's*

Mahogany Sidetable with marble top. English, mid-18th century.

193 *Hotspur Ltd.*

Carved mahogany console Table with marble top. English, about 1745.

194  *Christie's*

Mahogany Armchair with spoon back. The arms terminate in eagles' heads, the knees with lions' masks. English, about 1725.

195 *Sotheby's*

Bureau in burr walnut. English, about 1740.

196 *Sotheby's*

Carved and gilt console Table. English, about 1740.

197 *Christie's*

Mahogany Sidetable, attributed to Giles Grendey. English, about 1735.

198 *Frank Partridge & Sons*

Carved mahogany Chairs covered in yellow silk floral damask. English, mid-18th century.

199 *Frank Partridge & Sons*

Carved walnut Side-table; acanthus leaf decoration and claw and ball feet. A type more frequently seen in mahogany. English, about 1740.

200 *Victoria & Albert Museum*

Mahogany Bookcase with carved Corinthian pillars. English, about 1740.

201 & 202 *Mrs. Geoffrey Hart*

Table, with its top in silver gesso. English, about 1710.

203
Private Collection

204 *Christie's*

Mahogany Sidetable, possibly by Giles Grendey. English, about 1740.

203. Walnut Tallboy. English, about 1730.

205. The Supper Room. The Governor's Palace, Williamsburg, Virginia. Chinese wallpaper. The furniture mainly English from the early to the mid-18th century.

205

206 *Christie's*

Mahogany Commode by William Vile. English, about 1740.

207 *Frank Partridge & Sons*

Walnut bureau Cabinet. English, early 18th century.

From Mahogany to Satinwood

FROM BOULLE TO THE FRENCH REVOLUTION

In England from about 1730 the furniture trade begins to emerge from comparative anonymity. Some, though not many, cabinetmakers achieve outstanding prosperity, one or two lasting fame, mainly because they ventured into print. Of them Thomas Chippendale, the joiner's son from Otley, near Leeds, is deservedly the best known, partly because his famous *Director* of 1754 was the first important publication of its kind whatever the degree of his personal participation in its production, and partly because of the high quality of the furniture which can actually be proved to have come from his workshop in St. Martin's Lane. It is ironic to note that the finest of this documented furniture—that made for Harewood House for example—would hardly, on the evidence of the successive editions of the *Director*, be ascribed to him at all. But within a decade the patterns in this famous work were already out of date, Chippendale was cheerfully working to the designs of Robert Adam, and must be regarded not as a great innovator but as one fine maker among several of no less consequence, among them Giles Grendey, William Hallett, the pompous John Cobb, partner with William Vile, Robert Manwaring, William Ince and John Mayhew (in partnership), and George Hepplewhite. Ince and Mayhew, fired by Chippendale's example, published their *Universal System of Household Furniture* in 1759. Robert Manwaring published several design books. The Hepplewhite *The Cabinet-maker and Upholsterer's Guide* was published in 1788, two years after Hepplewhite's death. It is probable that of all the cabinetmakers of their day—when standards of material prosperity were improving and large numbers of "new men" were bent upon rising in the social scale—Vile and Cobb and William Hallett achieved the greatest success, though they never ventured into print. A number of fine pieces made by Vile and Cobb have been identified in Buckingham Palace. Hallett has left a very different sort of memorial. He made a more than considerable fortune, rebuilt Canons in Middlesex, once the mansion of the Duke of Chandos and lived there in splendid opulence. All that is forgotten, and the furniture from which that fortune came, has not, so far as I know, been identified. But he had his grandson and the latter's wife painted by Gainsborough; these two it is who walk magically together in Gainsborough's "The Morning Walk." London makers occasionally placed a trade label on their pieces; there was nothing like the fairly rigid Paris control, under which, by the middle of the 18th century, master cabinetmakers were required by their corporation to stamp their work with an iron—generally, in addition to their initials, the letters ME or JME for "Jurande des menuisiers-ébenistes." But even so there were certain exceptional men who had special privileges; among them Boulle and his sons at the Louvre until 1754 and Oeben and Riesener at the Arsenal. By this time the Gobelins had ceased to make furniture, but some workmen continued to occupy their old quarters and carried on independently. As to the prevailing styles in England throughout the century a foretaste of what could be accomplished by a man of talent was provided by William Kent (1685–1748) who can be said to have made things easier for Robert Adam a generation later by designing not only house and garden but all the interior decoration and furnishings as well. Holkham and Houghton among other great houses bear witness to his ability and a good deal of the grandiose, carved and gilded furniture made to his designs has survived. But while the influence of Kent was confined to the few, that of Robert Adam spread far and wide and into circles of too modest a fortune to employ him directly; few men can ever have left so lasting an imprint on their generation in the material sense, for his houses and those of his followers are scattered up and down the country and he dictated their characteristics from ceilings to fire irons. The year Chippendale published his *Director*, Robert Adam (1728–92) was in Italy; he absorbed the lessons of the past, studied the ruins of the palace of the Emperor Diocletian at Split in Dalmatia, drew ideas from Greek vases and Roman remains, noted the latest and best of the furniture fashions in Paris on the way home in 1758 and—in partnership with his two brothers James and William proceeded to the conquest of England. We are not concerned here with his architectural successes, but merely with his impact upon the cabinetmakers. In the twenty years between 1740 and 1760 they were all of them, as practical men of business, anxious to impress the world with their modernity and so—with a wary eye occasionally upon the sober past—they offered the public numerous rococo confections or the pseudo-Chinese already discussed, or the so-called Gothic style, wherein, for example, if a chair-back was composed of a painted arch or two, it was thereby romantically modish. All such things are engaging and beautifully put together, the carving crisp and lively. On all this Robert Adam imposed a salutary discipline, all the more valuable because it was largely indirect. Two good examples of "Gothic" chairs can be seen in Figs. 242 and 243.

A very graceful form of marquetry, based largely upon current French practice, came into favour for the first time since the early days of the century (e.g. Fig. 262); satinwood began to usurp the place of mahogany; painted panels sometimes took the place of marquetry and were presumably a good deal cheaper; the cabriole leg, for so long the mark of the finest chairs and side tables, disappears in England as it does in France. Instead, gracefully tapering square-cut legs, often reeded, are to be seen on some of the most distinguished furniture of the time, especially on those delicate little dressing or boudoir tables which the English makers copied from French examples, though without those refinements of marquetry or of the use of Sèvres porcelain or Wedgwood plaques which the average English taste finds so reprehensible in the more luxurious Paris pieces. Possibly the most original thing devised by the English trade towards the end of the century was the so-called Carlton House writing table, with its curved back, top surmounted by a pierced brass railing, and a series of drawers stepped upwards and backwards on each side of the writing embrasure. This was a type which remained popular for about thirty years, occasionally marred, unforgivably, by clumsily turned legs. The names of about 2,500 cabinet-makers, from the 17th to the early 18th century, are known; definite pieces, or a definite style can be assigned to a mere handful. To mention only a few, the furniture designed by Adam for Harewood House was executed by Chippendale, also some fine pieces at Nostell Priory. There are several pieces at Buckingham Palace by Vile, as already noticed; Gillows' of Lancaster sometimes stamped their work in the late 18th century, and some furniture is known bearing the trade label of Giles Grendey. There is a fine bureau in the Victoria and Albert Museum, in burr walnut and seaweed marquetry signed by Samuel Bennett (*d.* 1741).

In France, thanks to the method of stamping and to documentary evidence, numerous notable pieces can be assigned to individuals, while the dozen or so recognised leaders of the craft, many of them of German extraction, can be distinguished (though not without considerable study) by one or other of their personal mannerisms. The two sons of Boulle merely copy their father. Oeben, Boulle's pupil (1720–63), began the remarkable bureau à cylindre for Louis XV, now in the Louvre, which was completed by his disciple Riesener who married Oeben's widow and was destined to be ruined by the Revolution, with many others of his profession, and die poor and forgotten in 1806. If one can in any way describe a highly complicated matter in a word or two, one might say that the development of furniture from the early part of the reign of Louis XV until the revolution of 1789, when all the arts became more or less paralysed for a few years, is one of a gradual change from curves to rectangles, with a constantly renewed inventiveness and the most ingenious use of marquetry, lacquer and ormolu; indeed, for the greater part of the century, the bronze founders and chasers were no less important than the cabinet-makers. The results were pieces, sometimes of grandeur, sometimes of a delicate fragility, but invariably of an extremely luxurious character, by no means always to the taste or to the pockets of the English—nor for that matter, to those of the French beyond the narrow circle of the court, finance and the law. The point is that Paris drew to itself like a magnet the most gifted of craftsmen of Europe, and its prestige was so great that every princeling from Scandinavia to Switzerland longed to have about him something of the mingled grandeur and elegance of Versailles. When the great ones of the earth have those ambitions, lesser men follow suit as best they may. And some of the nicest things which have survived the passage of the years and the devastations of first the Revolutionary and Napoleonic Wars and then three separate German wars are the pieces from the French provinces, with a distinctly regional flavour, which follow the main lines of the furniture of Paris without its more luxurious extravagancies. This applies, both to what is now Belgium and to a lesser degree to Holland, which—on the whole—clung longer to its 17th century tradition of oak and walnut. Hepplewhite's *Guide* appeared in 1788, Thomas Sheraton's *Cabinet Maker and Upholsterer's Drawing Book* in 1791. Each went into 2nd and 3rd Editions. The former—an extremely sensible, practical book—contains a preface less laboured than was normal at this time, in which the following words occur: "English taste and workmanship have, of late years, been much sought for by surrounding nations; and the mutability of all things, but more especially of fashions, has rendered the labours of our predecessors in this line of little use; nay, at this day, they can only tend to mislead those Foreigners who seek a knowledge of English taste in the various articles of English furniture. . . . Though we lay no claim to extraordinary merit in our designs, we flatter ourselves they will be found serviceable to young workmen in general, and occasionally to more experienced men."

In spite of the good sense of many of his designs, it is unlikely that Sheraton ever had a workshop of his own, and it is a mistake to identify him—as was the custom a generation or so ago—wholly with satinwood furniture. He is a decided oddity, for who else, in designing a bed, could write: "As fancifulness seems most peculiar to the taste of females, I have therefore assigned the use of this bed for a single lady, though it will equally accommodate a single gentleman."

208 *Christie's*

Marquetry Commode, Louis XV, the panels inlaid with cube and trellis designs in kingwood and rosewood. French, about 1740.

209 *Christie's*

Marquetry Bureau. The sloping front encloses six small drawers, open shelves and a sliding panel. French, Louis XV, mid-18th century style of David Roentgen.

210 *Christie's*

Marquetry Commode. Various woods on a kingwood ground. French, Louis XV, mid-18th century.

211. Console Table in style of Thomas Johnson. Pseudo-Chinese carving, rustic branches and scrolling foliage (the base modern). English, mid-18th century.

211 *Christie's*

212 *The National Trust (Stourhead)*

Gilt carved Mirror; feathered female mask, pendant oak leaves. About 1740.

213 BY GRACIOUS PERMISSION OF H.M. THE QUEEN

213. Gilt carved Mirror – rococo style with floral pendants. One of a set formerly at Kensington Palace.

214 *Christie's*

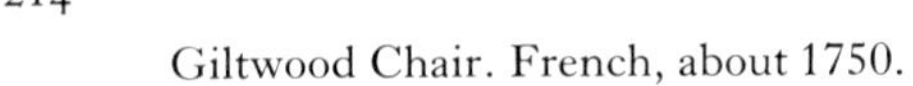

Giltwood Chair. French, about 1750.

215 *Christie's*

Carved mahogany Chair. English, the seats covered in contemporary needlework, dated 1747.

216. Burr-walnut Bureau-cabinet, the single door with damask-lined panel flanked by tapering pilasters. English, about 1720.

217. Bureau-cabinet. Red lacquer. Bears the trade label "Made by John Belchier at the Sun in St. Pauls Church Yard." Belchier died in 1753. English, *c.* 1735.

216 *Phillips, Son & Neal*

217 *Christie's*

218 *Sotheby's*

Mid-18th century mahogany Commode, probably by William Vile.

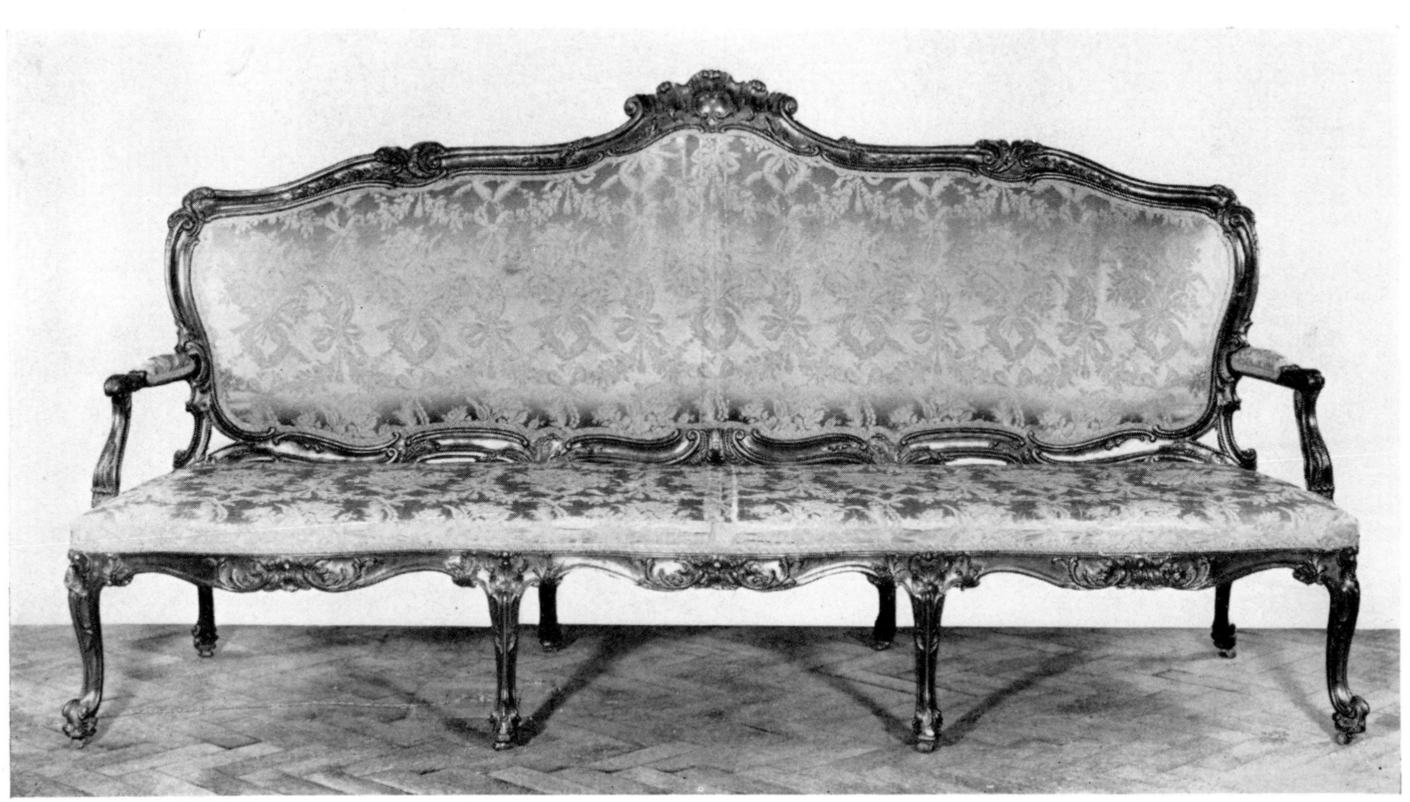

219 *Frank Partridge & Sons*

Settee, carved mahogany, 7 ft. 11 in. in length. English, and a superb example of the high standards achieved in the 1750's.

220 & 221 *Hotspur Ltd.*

Chippendale mahogany Torchère or candle stand with fret gallery top. Based on the design in Chippendale's *Director*. English, about 1760.

222 *Mallett & Son*

Chippendale style gilded and carved Mirror in the Chinese manner. English, mid-18th century.

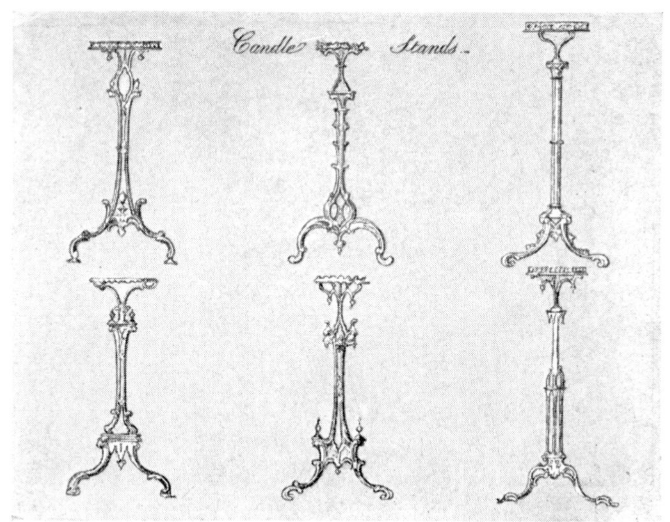

221 *Hotspur Ltd.*

223 *Hotspur Ltd.*

Two-tier Dumb Waiter, octagonal with fret galleries. English mahogany, about 1760.

224 *Hotspur Ltd.*

Carved mahogany Chair, Chippendale style. English mid-18th century.

225 *Hotspur Ltd.*

Mahogany silver Table, original fret gallery, stretchers and two pull out slides. English, Chippendale type, about 1760.

Victoria & Albert Museum

Painted wood Bedstead. Made for David Garrick at his villa at Hampton. English, about 1775.

227 *From a Royal Academy Exhibition*

Carved Mirror Frame in the Chippendale manner.

228 *Mallett & Son*

Carved and gilded Mirror. English, probably after 1750.

229 *A. Cook*

Chinese painted Mirror, carved and gilt frame, style in Chippendale.

230 *Sotheby's*

Another Chinese Mirror Picture in a carved English frame. Such mirrors as this and the preceding one were much appreciated imports from China during the last half of the 18th century.

231 *Sotheby's*

Roll-top Desk in tulipwood with ormolu mounts. French, Louis XV, about 1750.

232 *Frank Partridge & Sons*

Chippendale mahogany pedestal writing Table, the corners carved with flower garlands. English, the 1760s.

233 *Christie's*

Circular Table, kingwood and black lacquer, tapering legs. French, Louis XVI, about 1780.

234 *Christie's*

Rosewood and black lacquer *Bureau-de-Dame*, or boudoir writing Bureau, mounted with ormolu. French, Louis XV, about 1760.

235 *Christie's*

Black and gold lacquer *Bonheur-du-Jour*, with ormolu fretted gallery. The untranslatable *Bonheur-du-Jour* can be rendered soberly into English perhaps as a Boudoir Writing Table instead of "Happiness-of-the-day." French, Louis XVI, about 1780.

236 *Frank Partridge & Sons*

Fall-front writing Bureau, mounted in ormolu, with graceful floral marquetry. French, Louis XV, probably the 1750s.

237 *Christie's*

Mahogany Armchair, acanthus leaf carving. French scroll feet. A style derived from Paris. English, mid-18th century.

238 *Christie's*

Library Table, the panels veneered with kingwood on a rosewood ground, mounted in ormolu. By H. Hansen. French, Louis XV, about 1750.

239 *Christie's*

Library Table, mounted with ormolu and with floral marquetry. French, Louis XV, about 1750.

240 *Victoria & Albert Museum*

Carved mahogany Chair; the design is described in the third edition of Chippendale's *Director* of 1759 as a "French Chair." English, about 1760.

241 *Temple Newsam, Leeds*

Writing Table, made for Lord Crewe by Thomas Chippendale. Mahogany, with carved flowers mounted on satinwood. English, *c.* 1760.

242 *Victoria & Albert Museum*

Carved mahogany Chair in the "Gothic" manner. English, about 1760.

243 *Mallett & Son*

A "Windsor" Gothic Chair of yew wood. A rare country cousin of No. 242. English, about 1770.

244 *Sotheby's*

Pedestal writing Table, serpentine fronted, mahogany. English, mid-18th century.

245 *Frank Partridge & Sons*

Chippendale style mahogany writing Desk. English, about 1770.

246. So-called Carlton House Writing Table, mahogany. English. end of 18th century.

246 *Knight, Frank & Rutley*

247 *Sotheby's*

Library Table in kingwood, ormolu mounted. French, mid-18th century.

248 *Christie's*

French Library Table of about 1775, in contrast to No. 247.

249 *Victoria & Albert Museum*

Commode in floral marquetry of various woods, and mounted with ormolu, probably made in London during the 1760s. It has been suggested that this exceptionally fine piece of palace furniture may have been made by the famous Paris cabinetmaker of German extraction, Abraham Roentgen, who was here in 1766.

250 *Hotspur Ltd.*

Mahogany Commode in the French manner with ormolu mounts. English, the 1760s.

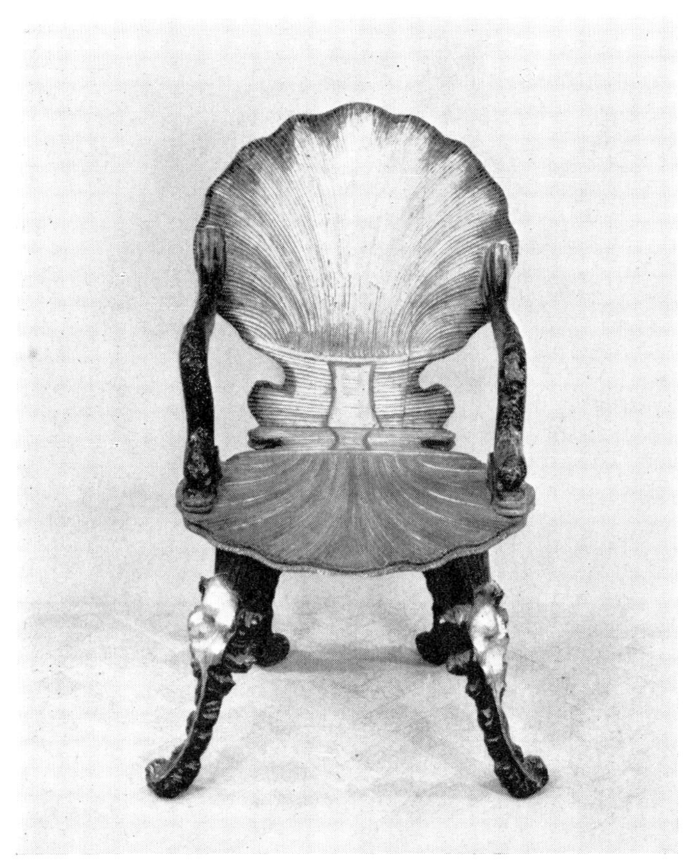

251 *Christie's*

Armchair, back and seat carved as shells. Dolphin arms and rustic legs, carved with rockwork and medallions, partly gilt and ebonised. Venetian, 18th century.

252 *Christie's*

Bamboo Chair, painted cream and light brown. English, end of the 18th century.

253 *Christie's*

Typical Chinese Chippendale mahogany Chair. English, about the 1760s.

254 *Christie's*

Chair, painted and gilt and carved in the shape of a swan holding a flower spray in its beak. Venetian, late 18th century.

255

Mallett & Son

Adam Bookcase in satinwood with urn and leaf marquetry. Domed cornice, carved wood swags on the glass doors. The lower part slightly serpentine. English, about 1780.

256 *Christie's*

"Ladder-back" Chair, mahogany. English, about 1775.

257 *Private Collection*

Mahogany Chair; an interesting continental variant of an English chair of Chippendale type. Possibly N. German, about 1775.

258 *H. C. Baxter & Sons*

Mahogany Chair with the graceful flowing lines associated with Robert Adam. English, about 1775.

259 *Jeremy's*

Mahogany Chair of about 1760 in the style Chippendale called "Grotto." English.

260 *Christie's*

Gueridon, or small circular Table, attributed to the cabinetmaker known by his initials only: R.V.L.C. Marquetry of various woods. French, mid-18th century.

261 *C. Lumb & Sons*

Mahogany Armchair, heart-shaped back, Prince of Wales' feathers, reeded tapering legs; typical Hepplewhite pattern. English, about 1780.

262 *Christie's*

Kidney-shaped Worktable of kingwood and marquetry of various woods. French, mid-18th century.

263 *M. Harris & Sons*

Mahogany Window Seat from the Gillow factory at Lancaster. English, about 1790.

264 *M. Harris & Sons*

Painted satinwood Sideboard. English, about 1790.

265 *M. Harris & Sons*

Marquetry Commode. An Adam design following French fashions, about 1775.

266 & 267 *Paris Sale*

Marquetry Table of about 1760, signed B.V.R.B. French.

Victoria & Albert Museum

An Adam Room from No. 5 Adelphi Terrace. English, about 1770.

269 *Hotspur Ltd.*

Three mahogany Chairs with unusual riband motif on the pierced backs. English, about 1770.

270 *Hotspur Ltd.*

Adam style knife Urn in carved mahogany. English, *c.* 1770.

271 *Hotspur Ltd.*

Carved mahogany wine Cistern on lion's paw feet, put to modern use. English *c.* 1750.

273 *Christie's*

Adam mahogany Armchair, the pierced lyre-shaped spalts carved with circular foliage medallions. Similar to a set designed for Osterley *c.* 1775 by Robert Adam.

272 *Mallett & Son*

An Adam Mirror of about 1780, with gilded metal frame.

274 *Hotspur Ltd.*

Carved mahogany Sideboard of Adam design. English, about 1780.

275 *Sotheby's*

Carved Chippendale Chair. English, about 1760.

276 *Hotspur Ltd.*

Mahogany Chair, late 18th century, style of Hepplewhite.

277 *Phillips, Son & Neale*

Mahogany Chairs in Adam style with lyre-shaped splat and fan cresting. English, late 18th century.

278 *Victoria & Albert Museum*

Adam Chair, one of a set designed by Robert Adam for the "eating-room" at Osterley. The original drawing is in the Soane Museum.

279 *Victoria & Albert Museum*

The "ladder-back" Chair of the 1760s in all its elegance.

280

Mahogany Armchair of about 1770 – a poor country cousin of the Chippendale style.

281 *Christie's*

Giltwood Chair covered in Aubusson tapestry. French, about 1780.

283 *Christie's*

Settee, made by Samuel Norman of Soho in 1764 from Robert Adam's designs.

282 *Victoria & Albert Museum*

282. Satinwood Chair, painted in colours; caned seat. Corresponds in all details to a set supplied to D. Tupper of Guernsey in 1770 by Seddon Sons & Shackleton.

284 *Frank Partridge & Sons*

Chair of carved and gilded wood covered in Beauvais tapestry, by George Jacob (1739-1814). French, about 1780.

285 *Frank Partridge & Sons*

Another variation on the same theme. French, about 1780.

286. Mirror, engraved and enclosed in moulded borders, enriched with flowers and foliage and ivy leaves in coloured glass. Venetian, late 18th century.

286 *Christie's*

287. Carved and giltwood oval Mirror in Chippendale style. English, the 1750s.

287 *M. Harris & Sons*

288 *Christie's*

A *Bonheur-du-Jour*, i.e., boudoir Writing Cabinet. Kingwood, inlaid with mahogany and satinwood. French, about 1760.

289 *Christie's*

A *Bonheur-du-Jour* translated into English. A satinwood Bureau by Gillow of Lancaster. Late 18th century.

290 *Sotheby's*

A marquetry writing and toilet Table. French, about 1760.

291 *M. Harris & Sons*

291 & 292. Late 18th century painted satinwood Sidetable. English.

292 *M. Harris & Sons*

293 *Frank Partridge & Sons*

294 *Mallett & Son*

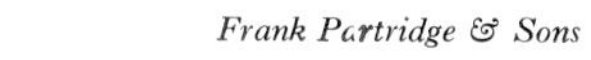

295 *Sotheby's*

293. Mahogany Urn Table. English, about 1775.

294. Mahogany Chair; Hepplewhite style in the French manner. English, about 1775.

295. *Secretaire à abattant*, i.e., fall-front Bureau with floral marquetry. French, about 1760.

296 *Christie's*

Giltwood Chair; Adam style in the French manner.

297 *Christie's*

Rosewood small circular Table (gueridon) veneered with king-wood. Marble top with pierced metal gallery. French, about 1770.

298 & 299. Two unusual Windsor Chairs.

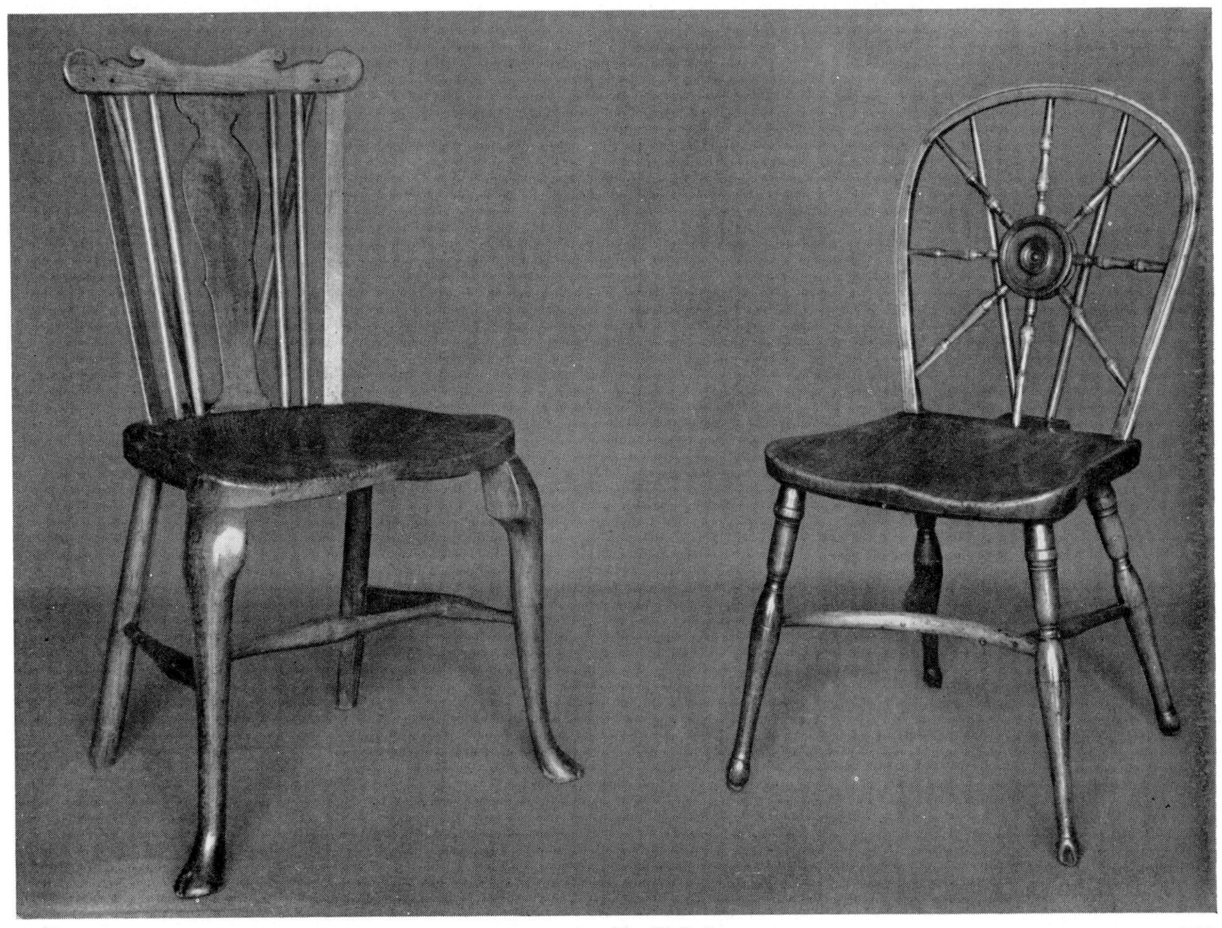

298 *Mrs. W. P. Ross* 299

300. Giltwood Chair covered with Beauvais tapestry. French, mid-18th century.

301. Kingwood Writing Table. Leather covered writing slide with recesses for ink, etc. Ormolu mounted with a pierced gallery. French, about 1780.

302. Small circular Table in the style of David Roentgen. French, about 1780.

300

301 *Christie's*

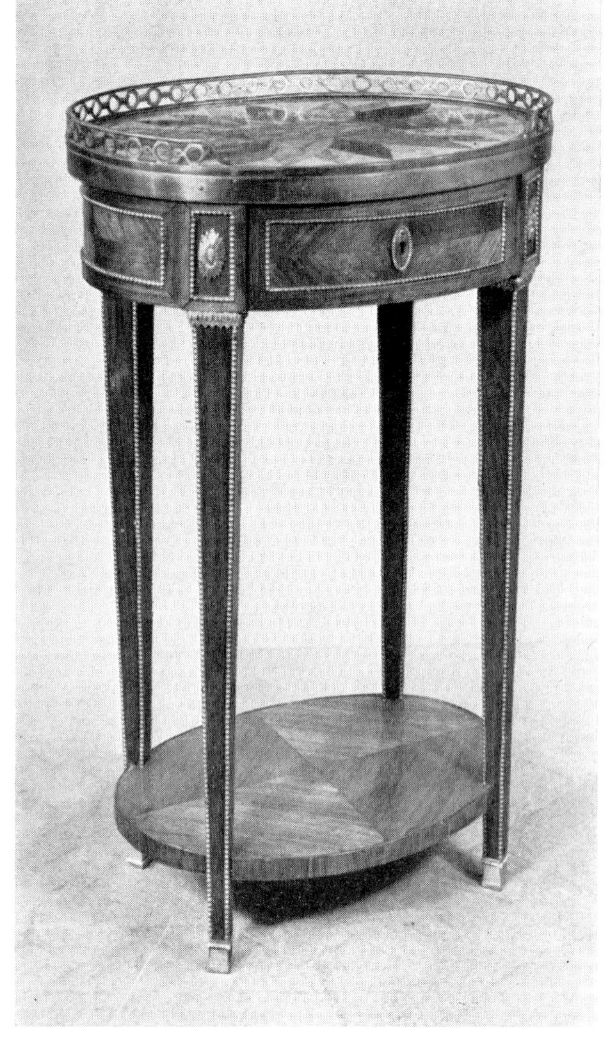

302 *Christie's*

303. Carved mahogany Armchair made for Nettlecombe, Somerset, in the 1760s, from Robert Adam's designs.

304. Chairs of carved mahogany. English, about 1760.

303 *Christie's*

304 *Christie's*

305. Mahogany Commode, ormolu mounted and with canted angles. French, by G. Beneman, court cabinet-maker in the 1780s.

306. Walnut Commode, with ormolu escutcheons and handles. French style. South German or Swiss, mid-18th century.

307. Satinwood, mahogany and various other woods. A Commode, probably by William Moore, of Dublin, once an employee of Mayhew and Ince, London, about 1792.

308. Mahogany wheelback carved Chair. English, about 1775.

305 *Christie's*

306 *Christie's*

307 *Christie's*

308 *Quinneys Ltd.*

309 *Frank Partridge & Sons*

Upright Secretaire inlaid with flowers and musical instruments. French, about 1780.

310 *M. Harris & Sons*

Circular Bookstand in mahogany, with five revolving tiers and brass paw feet. English, late 18th century.

311 *Christie's*

Upright Secretaire, inlaid in various woods on a kingwood ground within rosewood borders. French, about 1765. By L. Boudin.

312 *Christie's*

Small marquetry Commode. Strong French influence. Possibly Swedish, about 1765.

313 *Christie's*

314 *Christie's*

313. Mahogany Library Table in the style of Charles Cressent. French, about 1760.

314. Small marquetry Writing Table with lifting top and leather-covered writing slide, inlaid in various woods. French, about 1760.

315. Mahogany pedestal Writing Table with slight carving. English, about 1770.

315 *Christie's*

316 *Sotheby's*

Marquetry Table on slender chamfered cabriole legs, with writing slide and fitted writing drawer beneath. Interlaced branches in kingwood on a tulipwood ground, by J. Feverstein. French, about 1770.

317 *Christie's*

Mahogany winged secretaire Bookcase from Nettlecombe, Somerset. The 1760s.

318 *Morton Lee*

Console Table veneered with thuya wood. Ormolu mounts. Wedgwood porcelain plaques on the frieze. By Adam Weisweiler. French, about 1775.

319. Satinwood breakfront Cabinet on stand. Sheraton design, about 1790.

319 *Mallett & Son*

320 *Hotspur Ltd.*

Late 18th century mahogany Sideboard, attributed to Gillow of Lancaster. The centre entablatuie, carved in low relief, is a drawer. English, about 1790.

321 *Hotspur Ltd.*

Hepplewhite style mahogany Chairs of about 1785, English.

322 *Sotheby's*

Mahogany Chair of about 1770 in the French manner. English.

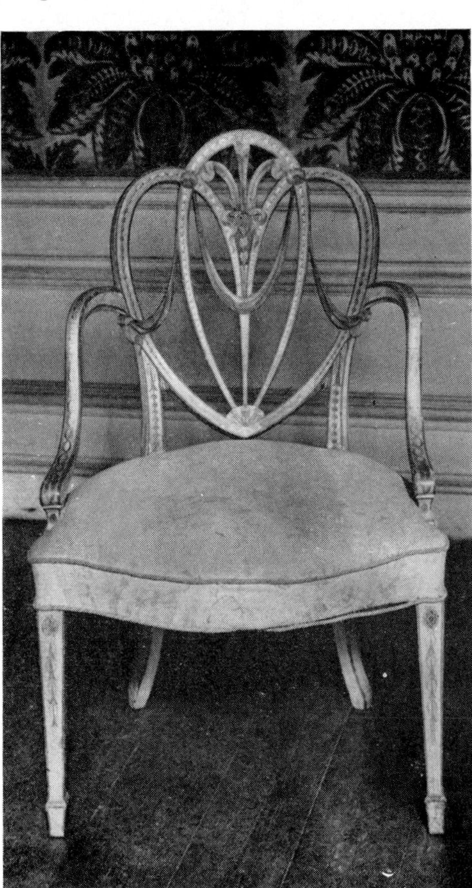

323 *Christchurch Mansion, Ipswich*

Painted and carved Chair, end of the 18th century. English, style of Hepplewhite.

324 *Phillips, Son, & Neale*

325 *Christie's*

326 *Leonard Knight*

324. Marquetry Bureau, mounted in ormolu. French, about 1770.

325. Mahogany writing Bureau; mid-century English.

326. Late 18th century roll-top writing Bureau. English.

327. Kingwood Commode with marble top and ormolu mounts. French, about 1780.

327 *Christie's*

328. Circular mahogany library Table, with 12 drawers and 4 angle cupboards. English, late 18th century.

328

M. Harris & Sons

329

M. Harris & Sons

Serpentine mahogany Chest of Drawers with carved canted angles. English, about 1770.

330 *Christie's*

331 *Victoria & Albert Museum*

330. Marquetry Writing Table inlaid with flowering plants and birds on a kingwood ground. French, about 1770.

331. Dressing Table with drawers, mahogany inlaid with satinwood. English, about 1780.

332. Sheraton type satinwood Writing Table, with movable silk firescreen, about 1790.

333. Small Writing Bureau, inlaid with a trellis design in mulberry wood borders. French, about 1770.

332 *M. Harris & Sons*

333 *Christie's*

334. Sheraton mahogany and satinwood Commode, cross banded in kingwood. About 1785.

334

Mallett & Son

335

Christie's

Marquetry combined Dressing and Writing Table. The top lifts up to reveal a toilet mirror, etc. The front is fitted with a writing slide. Marquetry of various woods, ivory and mother-of-pearl. French, provinces perhaps, about 1785.

336

Christie's

Carved mahogany Armchair, mid-18th century, in the French manner. The carved legs terminate in the French type of scroll feet. English.

337 *Norman Adams*

Mahogany Chair of about 1785.

338 *Frank Partridge & Sons*

Tulipwood Table, painted with floral panels at the sides. On the top a landscape in the style of Teniers. French, about 1785.

339 *Parke-Bernet Galleries, New York*

Late 18th century satinwood and sycamore Sidetable in the style of Robert Adam.

340 *E. T. Biggs & Sons*

Carved and gilt Mirror, mid-18th century, English.

341 *Christie's*

Carved and gilt oval Mirror, mid-18th century, English.

342

Painted satinwood Cabinet which once belonged to Richard Arkwright. English, towards 1800.

343 *Frank Partridge & Sons*

Carved mahogany Adam Sidetable of about 1775. English.

344 *M. Harris & Sons*

Mahogany Writing Table of the type known as "Carlton House" from the Prince Regent's Palace. English, towards 1800.

345 *Christie's*

Cabinet of satinwood and mahogany with marquetry designs of flowers and orientals. Towards 1800.

346 *Loewenthal*

Hepplewhite type mahogany marquetry Cabinet, about 1780.

347 *Temple Newsam, Leeds*

Mahogany Spinning Wheel. About 1790, English.

348 *Mallett & Son*

Mahogany Wine Cooler. English, about 1790.

349 *Christie's*

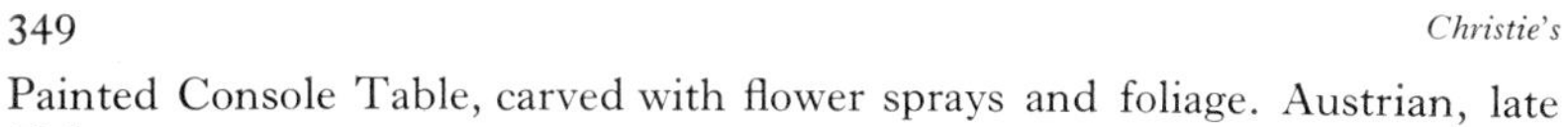

Painted Console Table, carved with flower sprays and foliage. Austrian, late 18th century.

350 *Private Collection*

Painted satinwood Chair with cane seat. English *c.* 1800. It was presented to an ancestor of the owner, in 1815, by the Prince Regent.

351 *Phillips of Hitchin*

Carved mahogany Armchair, probably from Chippendale's workshop and similar to the dining room chairs at Harewood House. English, about 1770.

352 *Christie's*

Painted Sidetable, carved and gilt with shell medallions, scrolls and foliage. Pale green ground. 18th century, Austrian.

353 *Christie's*

Carved mahogany Settee made for Nettlecombe Court, Somerset, to an Adam design. English, about the 1760s.

354 *Christie's*

Lacquer Plaque in an ormolu frame. French, mid-18th century.

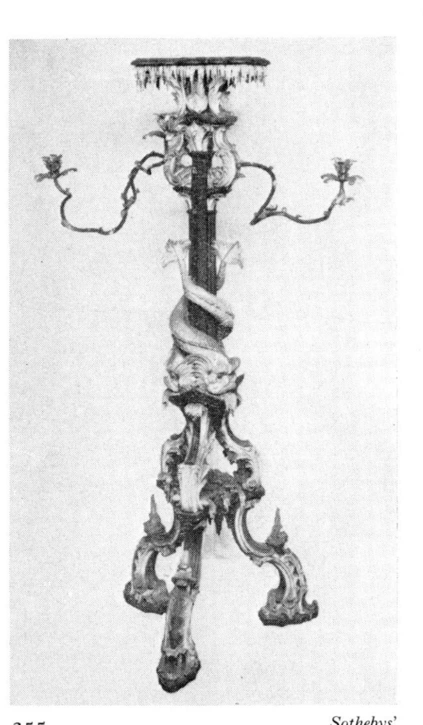

355 *Sothebys'*

Candlestand by Thomas Johnson. An elaborate whimsy of about 1760. English.

356 *Christie's*

Octagonal Mirror. Flower sprays and foliage in relief in coloured glass. Venetian, about 1770.

357 *Christie's*

Kingwood Cabinet by N. Petit – an example of the luxurious but simple style which became the fashion in Paris in the 1780s.

358 *Christie's*

Carved mahogany Tripod Table with circular tip-up top. English, about 1760.

359 *Col. J. M. Wadmore*

Painted satinwood Table with tip-up top. Style of Sheraton. The 1790s.

360 *H. Blairman & Sons*

Boudoir Writing Bureau. English, end of 18th century.

361 *Sotheby's*

Marquetry Tricoteuse or Worktable. Trellis pattern inlay, lyre-shaped end supports. French, about 1780.

362 *Hotspur Ltd.*

362. Mahogany Music Stand or "Canterbury." English, late 18th century.

The Nineteenth Century and After

Half a century or so ago it was almost an article of faith among the few who took an interest in such things that in France the whole craft of cabinet making was destroyed by the Revolution of 1789 and that in England nothing whatever of quality was produced after midnight on December 31st, 1800. We have since become somewhat less prejudiced and more tolerant. It would though be idle to pretend that as the years passed designers did not become heavy-handed and dull-witted. Probably the most cursory glance through the photographs which illustrate this section will be sufficient to show that from about the 1820's until the beginning of the 20th century furniture design was in the doldrums and has only recently begun to respond to the stimulation of new ideas. Each generation has its own notions of what is comely and fitting and it was inevitable therefore that in England by the 1790's the elegant formulas of Robert Adam should be wearing thin. The first man to attempt our conversion to new doctrines was Thomas Hope of Deepdene, a member of the great merchant house of Amsterdam, rich, eccentric and archaeologically learned, who, in 1807, published a fascinating volume entitled *Household Furniture and Interior Decoration* in which he abuses the past and advises his readers how persons of taste should furnish their houses. He speaks at some length of the general ignorance of the principles of visible beauty, of a few wretched conceits borrowed from the worst models of the degraded French school of the mid 18th century, and—in brief—accuses the cabinetmakers of enticing the wealthy to waste their money on rubbish. He goes on to advise a strict adherence to Egyptian and Greek prototypes and the results are seen in Figs. 368–372. He urges patrons to insist upon meticulous craftsmanship and provides a counsel of perfection useful only to those with unlimited resources. For that reason, if for no other, his influence was small; none the less a rather vague liking for Greek and Egyptian and Roman patterns was in the air, and George Smith in his *Household Furniture* 1808, illustrated some elaborate chairs with lion feet, Egyptian heads and various other devices, and followed this in 1826—he was upholsterer and furniture draughtsman to George IV—with another volume *The Cabinet-Makers' and Upholsterers' Guide*. Smith's point of view can best be described in his own words.

"It would appear almost unnecessary for invention to have gone further,"—he is referring to the work of the architect James Wyatt, who died in 1813—"but perfection, it appears, was reserved for the present period, in relation to ornament and domestic embellishment. In the year 1804 Mons. Denon's grand publication detailing the antiquities of Egypt became public. The travels of scientific men, the publications within the last twenty years, the Elgin marbles, all alike detailing the perfection of Grecian architecture and ornament; the beautiful specimens contained in Sir William Gell's work on the remains of Pompeii, the inexhaustible resources for beautiful outline in the vases of Sir William Hamilton, if no other causes had existed, would surely have been sufficient to account for the present elegant and refined taste."

It is perhaps unnecessary to note that once people have convinced themselves that a craft has reached perfection it is probably on the downward path. None the less the first quarter of the century produced many interesting and a few notable pieces. The most agreeable are probably those chairs with open backs and scimitar-shaped legs (generally referred to in the trade as Trafalgar chairs), and stools of X-frame construction derived from classical antiquity. Mahogany continued in favour, there was very little carving and even less marquetry, and satinwood was gradually discarded. Instead various other woods—rosewood and zebra wood (a striped wood from Guiana), amboyna and maple were used in combination with brass, the latter both as inlay and as wire lattice-work for the fronts of cabinets. There was even a well-known maker in the Boulle tradition, a certain Louis le Gaigneur of Queen Street off the Edgware Road. In addition there was a renewed vogue for things Chinese and Smith was careful to provide some designs "after the Gothic, or old English fashion and according to the costume of China." Clearly the cabinetmakers of the period were anxious to be all things to all men and had lost any sense of direction. Before long they were destined to lose whatever sense of proportion they may once have possessed, and in due course to have no ideas whatever beyond a slavish, and sometimes honest, imitation of the past. It is tempting to regard the tortured shapes of what was called Art Nouveau at the end of the century as mere aberrations (see Figs 395, 396, 397). No doubt they were, but they were also an attempt to evolve something new, and that must be placed to their credit. Although the French had descended to the same level of banality as ourselves by the 1840's, they produced some uncommonly dignified—some would say noble—furniture during the Napoleonic regime. The grace, the gaiety, the light-hearted experimentation had gone, but by no means the skill with ormolu and veneers. Of the majority of the famous cabinetmakers of the 1770's and 1780's we hear no more, but some few—notably the Jacob family—steered their way amid the perils of the tremendous social upheaval of the Revolution and adapted themselves to the demands of the new men. The tone of all the arts was one of high seriousness and when the pressure of events (and of course his own genius) made Napoleon master of the nation, a solemn sobriety was still the ideal. This was achieved—or at least attempted—by the cabinetmakers by means of a discreet use of gilded and chased ormolu in combination with large smooth surfaces of mahogany, the colour and beauty of the wood emphasised by the contrast between it and the matt surface of the gilded bronze—all this within a convention of severely rectilinear designs (side tables, cupboards, secretaires), the legs square. The more luxurious pieces are of solid mahogany, but exotic woods, thanks to the British blockade, were difficult to obtain, so the more normal method was to use thin mahogany veneers; for more ordinary pieces, all kinds of woods from poplar to elm and cedar. At this time the tall cheval glass makes its appearance both in France and England. Tables, large and small are mostly circular, supported by a central pillar or by three feet. The feet of tables and other furniture, the legs of chairs, the supports of bureaux are liable to have, either in carved and gilded wood, or in ormolu, some creature or other from the Græco-Roman-Egyptian mythology, in favour on both sides of the channel—sphinxes, winged lions, chimeras, sometimes as an integral part of the object, sometimes as if mounting guard on each side of it. Perhaps the period was least happy in its side tables, which tended to be oddly heavy, while the pretty little *bonheur-du-jour*—(the Happiness of the Day)—of the reign of Louis XVI grew into an alarming solid monster, formed, it would seem, by placing a rectangular box of pigeon holes upon a solid side table—an arrangement which has been described as an amalgam of the style of Louis XVI with that of the great oak pieces of the 16th century. As at other times England adapted some of these ideas in a modified form. Indeed, the general style of the English furniture discussed at the beginning of this chapter used to be called English Empire. It is now commonly referred to as Regency—and equally inaccurately, for the Prince of Wales only became Regent in 1811, and "Regency" is the normal word used to describe the varied but generally recognisable style current between about 1800 and the end of the reign of George IV in 1830. In addition to the chairs already mentioned one can find some extremely neat, elegant little open bookcases in mahogany or rosewood and some fine upstanding circular tables supported on a solid pillar; long three-pedestal dining tables with two spare leaves, the supports generally central turned columns with four curved brass legs.

A glance at the Catalogue of the Great Exhibition of 1851 is illuminating; never surely was wood so tortured, design so barbarously misused, commonsense so cheerfully thrown out of the window. Nearly everyone seems to have thought it all wonderful and a liking for knobs and incongruous excrescences is still endemic among a great part of the population if one may judge from some of the furniture in the shop windows in any industrial town. But a boy of 17, William Morris, also visited the Exhibition and disapproved; we owe him much, for later he was to play a notable part in the gradual emergence of the furniture trade, as of other trades, from the ungainly formulas of the mid century.

The last fifty years have witnessed a genuine renaissance in spite of two devastating wars and drastic economic change. It is no doubt rather early to attempt to assess the importance of these recent trends or to allot the credit for them to any one individual or group of individuals. One can perhaps say this. The Scandinavian countries have played a most important part in opening the eyes of all Europe to the possibilities, not just of the modern manner (a vague and nearly meaningless phrase), but of the comely manipulation of wood. So far, France, the unquestioned leader in these matters throughout Europe during the second half of the 17th and the whole of the 18th century, has done little more than follow suit. We can point with pride to certain pioneers of the not too distant past who by precept and practice led the way out of the rut. Two names spring to mind immediately; one the architect C. R. Mackintosh who designed the building and the furniture for the Conference Room at the Glasgow School of Art, illustrated in Fig. 399, the other the individual craftsman Ernest Gimson whose burr yew and mahogany chest of drawers of about the year 1905 is seen in Fig. 400. Sir Ambrose Heal is happily still with us and, of a younger generation, Sir Gordon Russell. It is doubtless true that we have the furniture as well as the government that we deserve; consequently that in the long run it is public taste which is the deciding factor. But the taste of the public has invariably been guided by the ideas of a few outstanding personalities and I would venture to suggest that, judging by the work now being produced by the leading members of the trade, both here and abroad, whoever compiles a furniture book of this sort one or two hundred years hence will be able to devote some very pleasant pages of illustrations to outstanding pieces of the mid 20th century which will stand comparison with the classic masterpieces of the 18th.

363 *Private Collection*

Carved mahogany Empire Chair, the arms supported by sphinx heads. French, about 1810.

364 *Christie's*

Giltwood and plaster Girandole, by Hay and Lyall, carvers to the Queen. Aberdeen, 1811.

365 *Christie's*

Ebonised Chair, the top panels painted in grisaille, cane and rushwork seats. Probably by John Gee, Turner and Chairmaker to His Majesty, No. 49 Wardour Street, 1803-17.

366 & 367 *Private Collection*

Two French Empire Chairs, one mahogany, the other beech or fruit wood.

368 *Photo: Tiranti*

A Room at Deepdene, Thomas Hope's mansion in Surrey. An illustration from his book, *Household Furniture*.

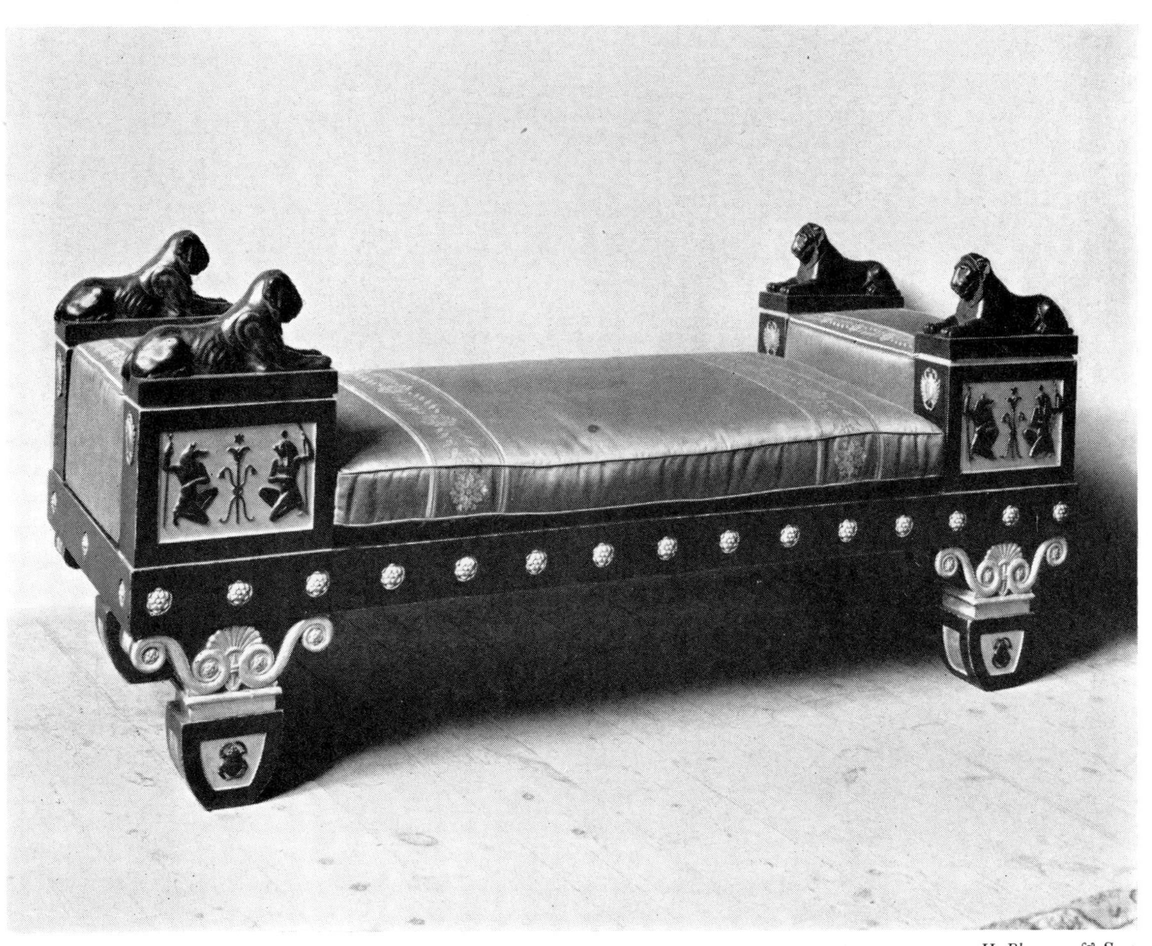

369 *H. Blairman & Sons*

The Settee from the Deepdene room.

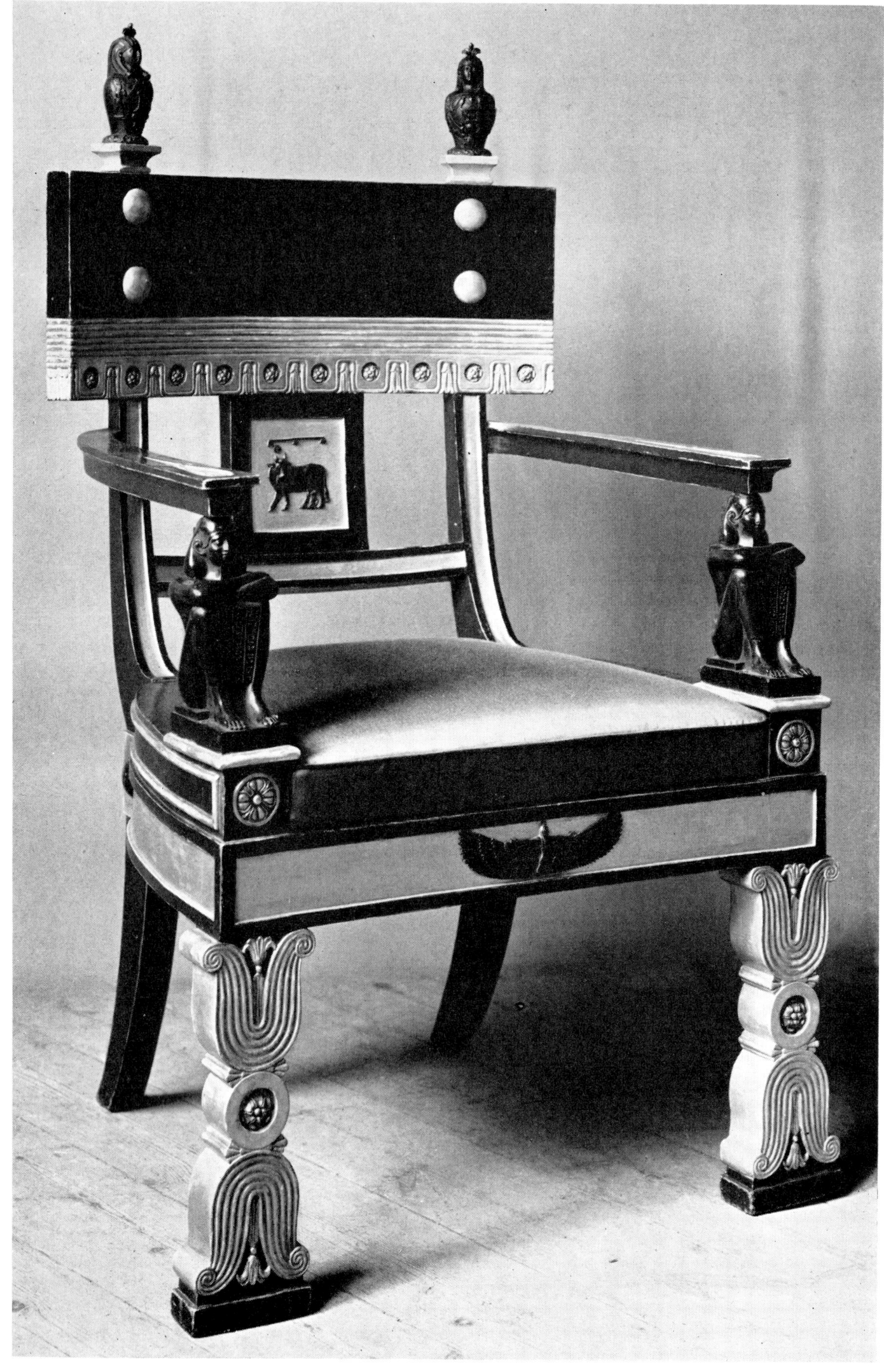

370 *H. Blairman & Sons*

One of the Chairs.

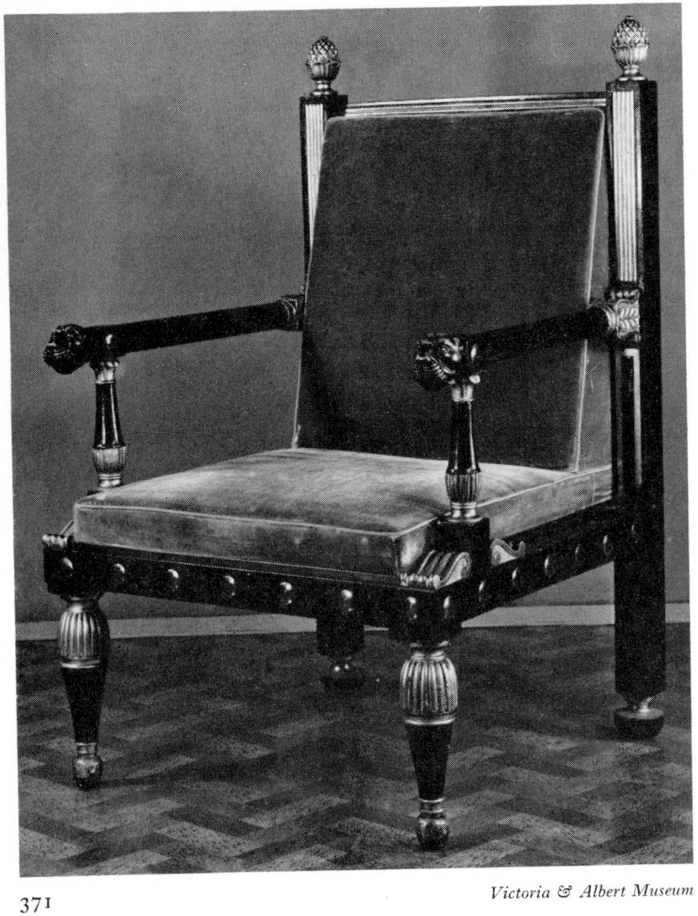

371 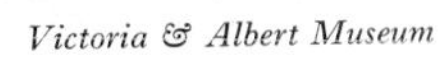 *Victoria & Albert Museum*

372 *Victoria & Albert Museum*

371. Another carved and painted Thomas Hope Chair.

372. A carved and painted beechwood Chair, obviously inspired by Thomas Hope's designs.

373. Typical Chair of about 1810. One of a set of six which were sold for £30 in 1910 and £200 in 1957.

373 *Knight, Frank & Rutley*

374 *Royal Pavilion, Brighton*

Mahogany Chair with gilt-brass ornament. Curved legs, straight seat rails and cane seat. English, about 1805.

375 *Victoria & Albert Museum*

Papier mâché and mother-of-pearl Chair. English, about 1860.

376 *Council of Industrial Design*

Mahogany Easy Chair of about 1860 – an adaptation with curious additions of a mid-18th century French chair. English.

377 *Council of Industrial Design*

A slightly less elaborate version of No. 376.

378

An early 19th century Sofa in the Royal Pavilion and a Cupboard made from panels of a Coromandel screen.

379

Imitation bamboo Cabinets and Chairs. The chairs were imported from China and bought for the Royal Pavilion, Brighton, in 1802. The cabinet (one of five) with panels of Japanese lacquer, was made for the Gallery of the Pavilion about the same year.

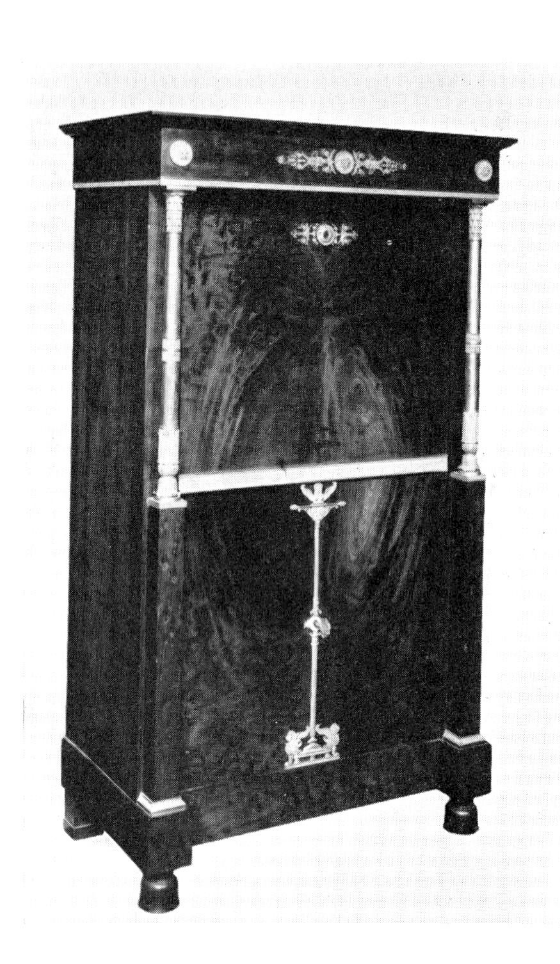

380

Private Collection

French Empire Bureau, mahogany with gilded bronze mounts. About 1805.

381

Rosewood Armchair. Cane seat, cane panel in back and turned front legs. English, about 1810.

382

Christie's

French Empire mahogany Commode with ormolu mounts. Stamped: Jacob D. and R. Meslee. This was the stamp used by F. H. Jacob on the death of his brother in 1803. He was employed in refurnishing Fontainebleau for Napoleon.

383

Mahogany Sofa or Pembroke Table. The sensible workaday table with a flap at each end, and often on two lyre-shaped supports, which came into favour at the end of the 18th century. This one could well be before 1800.

384 *Victoria & Albert Museum*

A palatial rosewood Commode. On the top and on the two drawers brass inlay in the manner of Boulle, a century before. The ormolu mounts are in the style of the French Regency and the engraving on the brass inlay round the doors is in the style of Robert Adam. English, probably the 1820s.

385 *Victoria & Albert Museum*

Another palatial Cabinet with brass inlay of about 1820. English.

386  *Pratt & Sons Ltd.*

387 *H. C. Baxter & Sons*

388 *H. C. Baxter & Sons*

386. Mahogany circular Table, early 19th century. English.

387. Rosewood Table showing variations in the supports. English.

388. Two small Tables with reeded legs. English, about 1800.

389. A further rosewood Table showing variations in the supports. English.

389 *M. Harris & Sons*

390 *Council of Industrial Design*

Mid-Victorian horsehair Sofa, used for the Sherlock Holmes Exhibition in 1951.

391

Circular Table by Owen Jones, made about 1872. Teak, inlaid with walnut, rosewood and sycamore.

Lent by the Home Office to the Exhibition of Victorian and Edwardian Decorative Arts at the Victoria & Albert Museum, 1952.

392

A room at Osborne House, showing a mid-19th century Sideboard and Sidetables.

393 *Victoria & Albert Museum*

English Cabinet of 1865, painted by H. S. Marks, R.A.

394. Oak Cabinet with inlay of various woods. Designed by John P. Geddon in 1861 with decorations by Burne-Jones.

394
Victoria & Albert Museum

396. An "art nouveau" walnut Chair. Designed by A. Darras and exhibited at the Paris Exhibition, 1900.

397. Another walnut Chair, designed by Louis Majorelle and exhibited at the Paris Exhibition, 1900.

395 *Musée Corbin, Nancy*

Bureau in the "art nouveau" style of 1900.

396 *Victoria & Albert Museum*

397 *Victoria & Albert Museum*

398 *Heal & Sons Ltd.*

Sideboard by Sir Ambrose Heal, 1929.

399 *Photo: Bedford Lemere & Co.*

Conference Room at the Glasgow School of Art. Both building and furniture were designed by the architect, C. R. Mackintosh, 1907-09.

400 *Victoria & Albert Museum*

400. Burr yew and mahogany Chest of Drawers, designed by Ernest Gimson about 1905.

401

401. Sideboard and Record Holder in mahogany. Designed by Walter Cornell, 1956, and made by Greaves & Thomas.

402

402. Sitting room Furniture, exhibited at Women's Fair, 1938, by Dunns of Bromley.

403 *Gordon Russell Ltd.*

403. Dining Chairs in solid mahogany or hardwood. Designed 1956 by W. H. Russell.

404. Windsor type "fan" Chairs designed by Sonna Rosen for Nässjö Stdfabrik, Sweden, 1950.

404

INDEX

Italic figures refer to Page numbers and Roman figures indicate Picture numbers